THE GENEROUS LEADER

THE
GENEROUS
LEADER

7 WAYS TO GIVE
OF YOURSELF FOR
EVERYONE'S GAIN

JOE DAVIS

BK®

Berrett–Koehler Publishers, Inc.

Berrett-Koehler Publishers, Inc.
1333 Broadway, Suite 1000
Oakland, CA 94612-1921
Tel: (510) 817-2277
Fax: (510) 817-2278
www.bkconnection.com

ORDERING INFORMATION

Quantity sales. Special discounts are available on quantity purchases by corporations, associations, and others. For details, contact the "Special Sales Department" at the Berrett-Koehler address above.
Individual sales. Berrett-Koehler publications are available through most bookstores. They can also be ordered directly from Berrett-Koehler: Tel: (800) 929-2929; Fax: (802) 864-7626; www.bkconnection.com.
Orders for college textbook/course adoption use. Please contact Berrett-Koehler:
Tel: (800) 929-2929; Fax: (802) 864-7626.

Distributed to the U.S. trade and internationally by Penguin Random House Publisher Services.

Berrett-Koehler and the BK logo are registered trademarks of Berrett-Koehler Publishers, Inc.

Printed in the United States of America

Berrett-Koehler books are printed on long-lasting acid-free paper. When it is available, we choose paper that has been manufactured by environmentally responsible processes. These may include using trees grown in sustainable forests, incorporating recycled paper, minimizing chlorine in bleaching, or recycling the energy produced at the paper mill.

Library of Congress Cataloging-in-Publication Data
Names: Davis, Joe., author.
Title: The generous leader : 7 ways to give of yourself for everyone's gain / Joe Davis.
Description: First Edition. | Oakland, CA : Berrett-Koehler Publishers, [2024] |
    Includes bibliographical references and index.
Identifiers: LCCN 2023038053 (print) | LCCN 2023038054 (ebook) |
    ISBN 9781523006618 (hardcover) | ISBN 9781523006625 (pdf) |
    ISBN 9781523006632 (epub)
Subjects: LCSH: Leadership. | Communication in management. |
    Employee motivation. | Interpersonal relations.
Classification: LCC HD57.7 .D39678 2024 (print) | LCC HD57.7 (ebook) |
    DDC 658.4/092—dc23/eng/20230828
LC record available at https://lccn.loc.gov/2023038053
LC ebook record available at https://lccn.loc.gov/2023038054

First Edition

31 30 29 28 27 26 25 24   10 9 8 7 6 5 4 3 2 1

Book production: Westchester Publishing Services
Cover design: Adrian Morgan
Author photo: Christopher Galluzzo, Sight and Sound Film, sightandsound.film

*This book is dedicated to
my wife of over forty years, Sarah,
who only knows how to engage with care and compassion;*

*my children and grandchildren,
who ensure I never lose sight of the power of the heart;
and*

*Sarah's dad, Richard Charles Nordholm,
who lived every day leading generously from the heart.*

CONTENTS

FOREWORD

By Fiona Hill

Humanity faces a series of existential crises, from climate change to pandemic to war. Our instinct at difficult times is to turn to leaders at all levels for guidance, reassurance, and empowerment. The quality of leadership and the values leaders demonstrate to their organizations and the world will inevitably determine our trajectory in the twenty-first century. Too often in recent years, authoritarian leaders, narcissists, and bullies have risen to the top. They hinder rather than help us overcome challenges. To succeed, we need thoughtful, conscientious, compassionate leaders, leaders who are generous in heart. There is no traditional curriculum to build these kinds of skills. They are not taught at business schools, but this book demonstrates that they can be developed through practice, self-reflection, and deliberate effort.

Joe Davis is a remarkable human being. I have known him for more than 20 years and have never failed to be impressed by his personal warmth and generosity. I have seen him in action at events large and small at the Boston Consulting Group, in his various capacities as the head of the Washington, DC, office, BCG's North

America operations, and in other regional and functional positions. I consider him a personal mentor, role model, and friend.

Joe is not the typical leader of a major company, and I am pleased to introduce the philosophy, lessons, and best practices that he has honed over his decades of leadership. This book, *The Generous Leader: 7 Ways to Give of Yourself for Everyone's Gain*, is more than a management guide: it is a unique and personal source of wisdom and inspiration from one of our era's great business leaders. It goes beyond mere strategies and the tactics of modern business—although there are great strategies and tactics discussed in the book—to talk about what really makes someone a leader worthy of respect whom employees will follow no matter how challenging the situation becomes. Joe's leadership philosophy, as detailed here, is focused not on technocratic management techniques but on the importance of generously building and maintaining character, trust, and communication within an organization.

Joe leads by example and empathy. He is deeply dedicated to the Boston Consulting Group, the teams he has forged, and the professionals whose careers he nurtured. He pays great care and attention to his colleagues. He is always focused on bringing out the best in people in a charged and competitive environment. Leaders are responsible for the success of their teams. Again and again, Joe has demonstrated that the most important thing a leader can do is freely give of themselves to help their employees thrive and reach their true potential.

The emphasis on care and compassion in leadership, which Joe describes so effectively in this book, could not be more important at such a difficult time in the United States. In recent years, what has passed for leadership at the highest levels of state has been cutthroat, often cruel and divisive, and at times unethical. The tone at the top has trickled down to all levels of society, including the workplace—where multiple studies highlight a prevalent sense of employee alienation. During the COVID-19 pandemic, this lack of a feeling of belonging led many Americans to reassess their priorities and leave their jobs.

The sudden frequency of phrases like "quiet quitting" and "burnout"—and the attendant need for better mental health support in the wake of the pandemic—is further evidence that companies and executives need to be doing more for their employees. With office strictures loosened and remote and hybrid work increasingly the norm in many contexts (while totally unavailable to workers in fields such as manufacturing), the need for empathetic leadership, strong cultural values, and clear communication is more acute than ever. It's no wonder that employees may be questioning their purpose and engagement when they see leaders behaving in questionable ways.

American workers in the lowest income brackets—those same people deemed essential during the pandemic—live precarious lives, paycheck to paycheck, without the time or stability to pursue education or grow in their careers. They expend their time and energy on survival. Workers are seeking new jobs in record numbers, while formerly beleaguered unions have gained new members and begun to re-flex their muscles. Employees want a say, and a stake, in what happens in the workplace. Empathetic leadership that considers the needs of workers can help change this sorry situation. Leaders model the behavior and values that infuse an organization from the top to the bottom.

As employees struggle with alienation, it is even more important for business leaders to build the authentic and personal connections this book describes. As I have observed Joe over the years, he has always prioritized creating the positive ties that bind people together and forging a sense of common purpose and commitment to a shared mission. It has been clear to me, observing leaders over my career and observing Joe in his roles, that building these connections is the key to effective leadership and to motivating teams. During the pandemic, Joe never wavered in his leadership of BCG North America—reaching out, connecting through frequent town hall videos. He "consulted" in the literal sense of the term, soliciting feedback and listening, not just informing colleagues after the fact of decisions that would affect them. Joe's example has always been one of treating people with dignity, respect, and honesty, and this has helped them thrive, innovate, and succeed. The results—the respect and success of BCG as a business—speak for themselves.

Joe's emphasis on the importance of empathetic leadership and character is not Pollyannaish. People face and struggle against enormous systemic challenges every day—from racism, discrimination, and poverty, to limited educational opportunities and access to basic services. I saw firsthand how hard it is to break systemic challenges growing up in the Northeast of England, in towns decimated by the successive shocks of war, mine closures, and deindustrialization. The out-of-work miners of County Durham certainly preferred a back-breaking job in the mines to no job at all, yet even when they were employed, it was in conditions that sapped them of their health and limited their horizons and their children's. At the same time, my experiences, career, and life trajectory, beyond the limitations of those communities and the circumstances I was born into, underline the fact that leaders can always act to break down barriers and even the playing field.

As I note in my book *There Is Nothing for You Here: Finding Opportunity in the Twenty-First Century*, CEOs and other executives—leaders of any large or influential organization—have an outsize ability to change outcomes and mitigate challenges for people individually and collectively. The more money, resources, and authority a person has, the more time they can dedicate to something other than survival and the greater the impact they can have. This is why it is critical for individuals in such privileged positions to act empathetically, model good character, and lead their organizations with integrity—just as Joe has always done. Leaders can create substantive change through mentorship, courageously confronting systemic bias, setting and achieving targets for hiring underrepresented people, and recruiting from a diverse range of institutions. In my experience, these are just a few concrete steps that any executive can take. The way leaders approach these sorts of actions and how they comport themselves communicates to their organizations—teams up and down the corporate ladder—that these activities are important and meaningful. How to do this effectively is, as I see it, one of the core elements of Joe's book.

One of my most vivid memories—vintage Joe—is of a holiday speech to the team, their families, and significant others after a particularly tough and demanding period for BCG. With Joe it's not just what he says but the way that he says it, the passion and spirit he brings to a speech that makes it resonate. Some might say that he wears his heart on his sleeve, but in fact he opens his heart to encourage others to do the same. He understands and embraces how everyone else is feeling. As he said on that occasion, "Step back, rest, take a breath, spend time with friends, family and with *yourself.*" In other words, if you don't care for yourself, you can't care for others. Joe's ethos is rooted in his love for his own family, which is always on display. He is never afraid to show affection, as well as his own vulnerability, and to express his feelings.

Joe's leadership style combines a broad mix of features—warmth and fellowship, gratitude for the contributions of others, the forthright recognition and acknowledgment of the pressures we all feel to perform, and compassion for the impact of stress (such as long working hours and travel) on personal lives. He never shies away from the difficult topics. Joe is always honest about why things matter. He addresses them head-on and validates the hard feelings—admitting to them himself: "I know I sometimes feel that way."

This honesty and transparency of feeling is part of what has made Joe so effective as a leader. These are also traits that can—indeed must—be honed and developed by leaders if there is any hope of success for their organizations or humanity's struggles against systemic, global challenges. In this book, Joe covers the most important traits for empathetic leaders in business. He explores the importance of personal connection, deep communication, perspective taking, and listening. With this foundation, true empowerment, allyship, and inclusive leadership become possible. But organizations must then convert ideas into action. As Joe outlines, this requires telling it like it is and noting and praising small acts, not just big successes. This creates a culture of mutual respect and reliable processes that bring greater success in the long term. These are soft skills, but they are the difference between good leaders and great leaders. Joe argues that we are all works in progress and that what we share with others and how we relate to them determines our ability to lead during good times and hard. Integrity—more than anything else—makes all the difference.

In this book, Joe offers practical perspectives and ideas that others can emulate and learn from. You will be inspired to do more in your own approach to leadership after you read it. Great achievements start with people. I am confident that the lessons and experiences Joe shares will not only help executives build successful work cultures and teams, but also form the foundation for the kind of leadership that will galvanize solutions to our world's most intractable problems.

THE GENEROUS LEADER

INTRODUCTION

You have come to this book to grow and develop as a leader (and, I hope, as a person). But what are you growing toward? What is the end goal? What is the shape of the CEO or C-suite member you seek to become? What are the skills you need to build to be this person?

There is a baseline assumption that you already have, or are developing, many of the basic skills, traits, and tools to be good at what you do and to be a good leader. And the marketplace is flooded with how-to books that can help you develop along these lines: Vision. Strategic thinking. Priority setting. Communications. Action planning. Metric setting to deliver results. This book cannot help you become a better stand-alone performer in those areas. This book is about the ways in which you can become a generous leader to be part of something *bigger than yourself.*

THE WORLD DEMANDS MORE

The old model for a leader—a top-down, unilateral, single-focus boss—isn't effective in today's workplace. That old model no longer attracts talent, invites collaboration, or gets the best results from the team. That leader's time has passed. Yes, change has been slow, but times *have* changed.

Why are these changes happening?

We are surrounded by disruption as a result of the growing and longer-term impact of technology, society's continued demands for social equality, and the obvious impacts of a pandemic.

Let's start with change driven by technology, beginning with the invention of the BlackBerry in 1999. The device improved productivity for the corporation because leaders could now easily be connected to their employees 24-7. But that meant the employee had to now be "on" 24-7. From the BlackBerry to the cell phone to the laptop and to Zoom, work has increasingly had access to us. There is, of course, much good that comes from this (convenience, work-location flexibility, access to data, and on and on), but the demands and expectations on employees have changed as a result. The work-life line has blurred, and our work life has become much of our day. The people with whom we work have now become critical in every moment of our day, not just the business hours—and with so much time spent at work, today's employees are looking to their leaders to have more than just professional ties. They want and need to connect in different ways.

The social media explosion and constant access to information has also elevated the need for leaders to reassure and guide, because people at work can feel in a constant state of uncertainty. Any stressful public event elicits common reactions from most—alarm, anxiety, fear, concern for one's job, worry about others, and so on. Today these events—whether they be reporting on climate change, alarming newsworthy events such as the January 6 attack on the US Capitol, the Russian invasion of Ukraine, or stressful statements and actions from world leaders—are instantly accessible, pushed to newsfeeds on our phones and computer screens. As people react to these happenings, leaders, of course, have to calmly use their heads, think through how their teams or organizations should react, and strive to protect their shareholders, their customers, and their employees. There's a sense of urgency as the inevitability of these events and their frequency amplifies the impact on all of us.

The growth of AI will only perpetuate, or accelerate, the disconnections created by that first BlackBerry and all the cell phones and social media platforms that followed. Whether it be Jasper or Chat-GPT (or the newest iteration of the tools) eliminating much of the white-collar workload, or "digital twins" taking on more and more real human-connection moments, AI will change the workforce. People will lose jobs during the transition, machines will enable fewer personal connections along the journey of solving problems, and we will grow more distant from one another . . . but we will still yearn for real connections. More than ever. The expectations that leaders should hold together a company culture as people are continually transitioning, should connect more personally with employees, and should show real care and compassion will only grow.

According to Kristin Peck, the CEO of Zoetis, today's collective workforce embraces an intangible drive, a need, for something more than any workforce in the past.[1] In an interview with *Fortune* magazine, she notes that millennials, who represent 50 percent of today's workforce, want to work for organizations where the leadership shares their values. But Peck also observes that there's another key trait this workforce seeks from leaders: "They want people who are more empathetic, who really engage with them in a very different way and communicate in a different way."

Leadership will require skills beyond the basic and traditional methods to manage through these profound transitions and changes. Reacting with the head is no longer enough. There is a need for a more human-centered, bighearted, authentic way to lead. And in this book you will learn to become the kind of generous leader the world needs.

A PEEK INSIDE THIS BOOK

There isn't a straight line to the end result you are looking for, and this can feel scary because leading with the head seems safe—it's justifiable, it's quantifiable, it's defensible—while leading with the heart feels like a "soft" alternative. I get it; I'm a numbers guy, looking for—and sometimes hiding behind—numbers. Like other leaders, I have sometimes had trouble getting out of my own way.

But I have learned that numbers can only get you so far. At some point, you must build the skills to connect with people to grow as a manager, leader, and person. The good news is that you have worked extremely hard to get where you are today—and you are driven to succeed. You *can* develop yourself further. And you *should*.

Samir Bodas, CEO of Icertis, has had a long career since leaving the Wharton School some 30 years ago. He worked at Microsoft through multiple leaders, led a turnaround in a post-Microsoft role, and started a couple of companies of his own. In describing his personal journey, he admits that he lacked empathy—he didn't even know what it was—when he came out of Wharton. It was all about numbers and money and having to deliver. Then, as he drove a successful company turnaround, and all that it entailed, he started to expand his thinking: "It may sound funny, but I started to practice metacognition. I began to look in my heart and see who I was. Why was I thinking as I was? Why was I saying this or that; what was I trading off? I began to test my values—where are they good, where should I change? I began to lead more with the heart."

He notes that it became an evolutionary journey for him, and he describes how he now sits down at the end of each year and asks himself several questions: *How am I a better leader? How am I a better husband? A better father? Am I a better human being? Where can I push further?* He admits that if the answer to the last question is a short list, then he knows that he's "being arrogant" and his "mind is getting in the way."

In the following chapters, you'll be introduced to the seven essential elements that I believe will develop *you* into a leader for the future. For me, they serve as an internal compass, a North Star, which guides my every day.

1. Connecting personally and deeply, becoming a generous communicator.
2. Being curious, listening to learn, becoming a generous listener.
3. Welcoming everyone, generously including many.
4. Standing up for others, becoming a generous action ally.
5. Growing others with recognition and feedback, becoming a generous developer.
6. Making small acts that will have big impacts, generous moments.
7. Being vulnerable, crossing your own line, giving up the mask.

In Chapter 9, Change Yourself: Be Generous in Your Own Personal Growth, we'll explore how we are all works in progress and need to start making changes now as we go deeper into our own journeys.

You'll hear from many other successful leaders about how they embraced their own humanity, alongside their intellect and experience, including Joaquin Duato, chairman and CEO of Johnson & Johnson; Joanne Crevoiserat, CEO of Tapestry (think Coach, Kate Spade, and Stuart Weitzman brands); Christine Gregoire, CEO of Challenge Seattle and former Washington State governor; Scott Kirby, CEO of United Airlines; Steve Gunby, president and CEO of FTI Consulting; and Christina Sistrunk, former CEO of Aera Energy (for all these executives, and others you will meet throughout this book, their thoughts and quotes are from my personal conversations with each). You'll discover how caring about the people you work with can enhance productivity and otherwise positively influence your results, your teams, and your organization.

We'll also explore some of the challenges that can get in your way and strategies for adapting your skill set and work style in order to evolve your leadership practices. Each chapter will leave you with some clear calls to action to get you started.

It is my hope that, at a very personal level, you will find this change in leadership style to be hugely satisfying. It will feel good!

THE FORMULA FOR SUCCESS: ELEVATE THE HEART

You may have heard about leading with the head, heart, and hands. My colleague Jim Hemerling helped popularize this school of thought in his book *Beyond Great: Nine Strategies for Thriving in an Era of Social Tension, Economic Nationalism, and Technological Revolution*, which he coauthored with Arindam Bhattacharya and Nikolaus Lang. It is thoughtful and spot-on, but, based on my years of experience, the disruptions currently affecting us, and the changing workforce expectations, I believe it is time we elevate the importance of a heart-led leadership style in order to adapt to the sense of urgency we are all experiencing and the inevitable crises to come. While I will not be so bold as to change a well-used phrase, I do believe one must lead with the heart—keeping generosity the key consideration in all decisions and actions.

What does it mean to lead with the heart? A Boston Consulting Group (BCG) / BVA Group global survey among 9,000 participants found that the top four leadership qualities valued by employees are those that emphasize the importance of leading with the heart (versus the "head" strategy or "hand" action interpretation of the

Hemerling book): recognition, coaching and development, empathetic listening, and care.[2] Jim also coauthored the article "Why the World Needs Generative Leaders," which notes that a generative leader is one who strives to leave the world a better place than they found it. Generative leaders are normally thought to lead equally with their heads, their hearts, and their hands, bringing the heart much more fully into the picture than has been common. Generative leadership is talking about what the acts of generosity yield—the results of being generous, and there are many.

This idea of leading with humanity—leading from the heart—sounds like it's all rainbows and unicorns; it sounds like "soft" skills, as we analytical consulting types would say. But, reader, here's the not-so-dirty secret: leading with humanity also yields better tangible results for you, your team, and your organization. Admittedly, this concept might be novel to some leaders. And it might be frightening to others, especially since it's so contrary to the leadership styles found in yesterday's C-suites. This book is designed to help you assess and reframe *your* leadership style to elevate and lead with your heart in order to generate results.

But the central point of this book is not to act generously solely in order to achieve results. There's a critical distinction. Yes, I believe these generous acts are the key to your success—it's why I'm writing this and a major reason why those interviewed, and I, have been so successful—but they should not be the real motivation for the actions. Generosity, by definition, is an act that is "given freely" without expectation of benefit for the giver.

Finally, it should be noted that within the pages of this book, when I talk about "generosity," I am not speaking about remuneration. Equitable compensation should absolutely be a mandate in every organization, but that is not the subject of this book.

THE GENEROUS LEADER

This book is about unlocking the best parts of yourself to become the best leader you can be. It is about finding ways to give and do and be for others, knowing that the results are generative, but the motivations are generous. Collaborating, showing respect, giving recognition, exhibiting humility, providing validation, paying close attention, ensuring accessibility, doing for others—these are the acts of a generous leader. A generous leader must be committed to diversity, equity, and inclusion—it cannot be said with enough emphasis. Showing deep compassion with core values that clearly articulate equality, inclusion, and fairness is key. Meeting these demands is the right thing to do.

Executing the heartfelt practice of inclusion and building and supporting a diverse team is not simply about hitting metrics; nor is it about your own conscience. It is good for your business. It is the right thing to do for individuals who may be facing structural disadvantages. It is the right thing to do for humanity. As you build and support a diverse team, incorporating insights and experiences from many, while solving tough problems, you'll wind up with a richer set of options, a better understanding of the critical obstacles to overcome, and, with that, better results.

WHY ME?

I have had more than 40 years of experience managing and leading teams, having started in my early 20s as a sales rep, then a manager of three sales reps at Procter & Gamble, and finished as the head of BCG North America, leading a 7,000-plus-employee business. Throughout my career, I have opened new offices and new businesses, and I've navigated many turbulent times: the dot-com crisis, 9/11, the American war in Iraq, the Great Recession of 2008, and the on-going COVID-19 pandemic—to name a few dramatic disruptions. I also have the privilege of serving as the chair of BCG's Center for Inclusion and Equity and am a founding steering committee member of CEO Action for Racial Equity. All of these experiences across roles and geographies have helped me see the many ways that hardship can affect employees and their families and how yesterday's rigid, profit-oriented leadership styles served as more of an encumbrance than a springboard to growth and success. I discovered the necessity of becoming a leader who cares deeply about my teams and my colleagues, and in so doing, I saw firsthand the value of leading with care and compassion.

Along the way, I also gained access to dozens of other high-level professionals and thousands of regular "Joes" (pun intended—we were all once regular Joes). They, too, learned the hard lessons over these past several decades and came to recognize the value of compassionate leadership. With the help of these colleagues, I developed the belief that it's finding the commonality between all of us, and connecting through it, that is at the core of our best humanity.

Now it's time for *you* to learn how to elevate your heart, lead with humanity, and live a life of deep integrity. Let's get started!

1

GENEROUS LEADERSHIP, DEFINED

I was on a plane, the regular shuttle between Boston and Washington, DC, sitting next to Steve, who had been my mentor since the day I joined BCG. We were in the bulkhead seats, on the right side of the plane. Yes, I do recall this detail; it was a vivid moment for me.

He and I were on our way to DC to house hunt and open BCG's Washington, DC, office, an office that had been a year in the planning. He was a senior partner; I was a manager at the time. I had already moved my family to DC to start two of my children in school. Steve and his spouse were going to follow sometime in the fall.

Our plane took off, and we were on our way when Steve looked over at me.

"Joe, rather than risk you hearing this secondhand, I wanted to let you know I got a job offer—to be president of another company."

I froze. You can only imagine what flew through my mind. *Oh crap, what does this mean for me? I have already moved my family to DC! Am I going to displace my family again? What am I going to tell Sarah, my wife? Will I be losing my mentor?*

I replied, without much hesitation or expression, "Great, real proud of you, that is cool." Still wondering, *What the hell?*

Steve had glanced out the window but now looked over at me again. "Don't sweat it—of course I decided not to take it." He explained, "There are many puts and takes, but part of it is that there is no way I was going to do that to you and Sarah. You have moved your family to join me in opening this office—how would I ever take that job? I just wanted to make sure you didn't hear about it secondhand and worry."

Wow! What a powerful moment for me in these early years of my business career. Steve was forgoing an opportunity to lead a company as president—along with the compensation upside, the cachet, and the status that come with such a title.

He cared deeply about what he was starting with me, about the commitment he'd made to me. He cared about the impact on my family. While I am sure there were multiple reasons for his decision, the one that mattered to me was that he cared enough to not disrupt my family. Talk about having one's back, about generously considering another in important moments, about leading with care.

This was a meaningful moment for me—in my early 30s, a few years into a new career, speaking with a leader who was known to be extremely results focused. In that moment, that leader considered the impact of his decisions on another's life and, as I saw it, put *my* family first. Over 35 years later I still vividly recall that plane ride and that experience of generous leadership.

THE OLD MODEL—GENEROUS TO WHOM?

Leaders have always been celebrated for the results they deliver. But what results? For many years they were single focused: in the business world, shareholder returns; in the government, growth; in the nonprofit space, funds raised—all done, of course, while delivering the organization's mission.

What were the actions and traits called out that delivered those results? Being number one, two, or three in your sector. High-quality products or services, absolutely meeting customers' needs. Highly efficient operations. But also cutthroat focus on delivering that efficiency. Staffing an organization that dutifully drove to the desired results. (How many white shirts and dark-blue suits did one see on the streets of our major business centers?) A leadership-centric, almost selfish, behavior from the boss.

The often-cited heroes of business drove the numbers, led from the top, built command-and-control organizations, let metrics and statistics drive nearly all decisions, made tough calls with a single lens: dollar profit. An almost impersonal, cutthroat "tough leader" somewhere along the way became synonymous with effective and "great." Aspiring leaders sought to build themselves in this image.

There have, of course, been many great leaders across time, those who were deeply admired and respected for taking a broad view of their mandate, who focused on the numbers but also cared deeply for their people and were concerned about their company's impact on the community. They existed, but this type of generous leader, who saw "their people" as humans, who led with care and compassion, who put their heart in the front of their leadership, was rarely visible. More to the point, this broad view of leadership was not in fashion, received less attention and fewer accolades, and as a result was not considered a model for success.

IT IS NOT ABOUT THE MONEY

I want to be very clear that I am not defining the generous leader as one who offers their employees an incredible pay package. As I have said, this kind of generosity is not about remuneration.

However, when you are invested in another person's well-being, you work hard to help them develop professionally. In Chapter 6, Recognition and Feedback: Generous Development, you will learn specifically how to do this in a pointed but also beneficial way. This development can and often does lead to promotion and career advancement, and therefore a possible indirect result of your generous leadership is, in fact, about the money. That is the generative result of generously devoting your time and attention to another person's professional growth.

CHANGE DOESN'T HAPPEN OVERNIGHT

As I noted in the introduction, there has been a change afoot, which has accelerated in recent years. Expectations of a great leader have evolved.

Fran Katsoudas, EVP and chief people, policy, and purpose officer of Cisco, shared with me how, early in her career, she had received feedback warning her to avoid being too caring or compassionate. Someone actually pulled her aside and said she needed to develop more of a *killer instinct*. "Do not care as much," she was told. "You will do well if you put some of that away." But she knew that expectations would be changing, and she took a different approach.

> I didn't follow that advice because it wasn't authentic to me. In the end, the approach didn't work well for the leader, and it wouldn't work well for leaders today either. I will make tough decisions, engage with intense issues, and ask how fast we can move, but I will always strive to do so with respect and caring.
>
> A clear shift has been underway in the workplace. Empathy is needed more at this moment than any other time.

This change did not, of course, happen overnight. As Fran said, it has been evolving. As the demands on each of us have changed, so too have our expectations of our work life, and our leaders. Our work and life hours, and locations, have blurred so much that, for most, you cannot be one person "at work" (as unsatisfying as even that may have been) and then a more human you "at home." You want to feel as human, as seen, as fulfilled in your now ever-on work life as you had striven to be outside work.

In addition, the pressures and anxieties of our ever-complicating world, made much more immediate by social media, result in new expectations of leaders. Yes, they must represent their organization, and they must deliver results. But today there is an imperative to do more: to generously give of themselves to nurture and inspire all people within the organization, and to contribute to the greater community.

WHAT MAKES A GENEROUS LEADER

Generous is defined by the *Cambridge Dictionary* as willing to give help, kindness, etc., especially more than is usual or expected. I cannot emphasize enough the importance of giving this help without thought of benefit to oneself, and doing it with the reflexivity it requires, which is how I interpret this definition. It also calls to mind the lately overused word *authentic*, and I do believe that the essence of the giver must be completely authentic in order for these acts to be interpreted as intended, as truly generous.

As is often attributed to Aristotle, "We are what we repeatedly do. Excellence, then, is not an act but a habit." Much of the work in this book, as we talk through the potential challenges you may face, will be developing self-awareness and your own skills to do this instinctively and without reservation. It is not just the giving of one-self; it is also about doing it without hesitation. It is about the excellence that comes with habit. It is a big ask. It takes practice for it to become a habit.

For example, as I write this in June 2023, the airline industry just had a horrible week of flight cancellations driven by severe weather and an antiquated and short-staffed US aviation oversight system. Scott Kirby, United Airlines CEO, came out at the end of the week in an all-staff email to say, "I want to say thank-you for the incredible work," and tell the team, "I want you to know that I'm proud of you." You may think, OK, thanking the team after a hard week, so what? But Scott makes it a daily practice, and there are countless examples.

Connect deeply and personally with your colleagues. Show humility, be genuine and caring. Listen to others, truly aiming to understand their perspectives and to uncover from them what you do not know. Find opportunities to learn from them. Really see your people and make them feel seen. Recognize their contributions, leverage their strengths for their own advancement, and push them, honestly and directly, to be more than they believed possible. By infusing your heart, and your humanity, into your leadership style, you will become a more generous leader, and the people you manage will become free to perform at their best. The ultimate outcome will be more effective contributions from all to your organization's purpose and mission.

2

CONNECT PERSONALLY AND DEEPLY

Generous Communication

Communicating to connect may not come naturally, especially as we start our careers; we think more about conveying the information and facts we believe we must get across. But I will argue that you can get those facts across and still be true to yourself and your message. In fact, with all the skepticism out there, communicating that you care and making deep personal connections when delivering important messages is essential to building better-connected teams. This becomes essential to leading your organization to greatness, given that you cannot, of course, do it alone.

TAKING A CHANCE

It was the start of the pandemic.

I woke up at 4:30 on a Thursday morning, about two weeks into the new work-at-home model, concerned about our people and their personal situations. My mind was racing for all 7,000 of them, and I started thinking about what I would like to say to them. *How can I connect with them, personally, in this moment?* I wanted them to feel less alone. I wanted them to feel less scared. I wanted them to feel valued. And I wanted to be real. I climbed out of bed and wrote how I felt for them.

From: Davis, Joe
Sent: Thursday, March 26, 2020, 5:16 a.m.
To: All Staff
Subject: Good morning

I woke up this morning thinking of each of you, whether you are living:

In a small city apartment with multiple roommates.

By yourself.

As a couple navigating new "office" space in the bedroom and living room.

As a family tripping over children, or dogs, or children and dogs.

In all the combinations we can imagine.

I admire you:

For your connections to one another.

For your commitment to your friends and families.

For your contributions to BCG and all that we each try to do every day to make a difference.

For your willingness to keep at it.

I am honored you are my colleagues.

I hope you each have a wonderful day.

Joe

(This is a personal note, as I was awakening this morning.)

I spent 45 minutes writing and rewriting the brief email, carefully considering each word as I imagined the likely reactions from everyone as they read each sentence, and debating, in my own mind, what to do. *Should I send such a personal note?*

I wanted the words to be perfect. I wanted to lift everyone up. I did not want to wallow in negativity. At the same time, I was also wondering about how they might respond. *Who do I think I am to presume to know, or even to guess, how they are feeling at a time like this?*

I also wondered what my fellow corporate officers might think: *Who does he think he is to get so personal?* I worried they'd feel I was putting pressure on them to engage with their own people more deeply.

Would this note diminish me as the "in-charge" leader people hoped for, and expected, in this moment of growing crisis? Or would they think I was nuts waking up thinking about them at 4:30 a.m.? Would this send an unwanted signal that I expected others to be up working long before sunrise?

Most basically: Who sends such personal notes to 7,000 people? I pressed Send and let it fly.

The response was overwhelming and heartwarming, and it confirmed that the compassion I felt was appropriate and landed the way I intended. One employee who thanked me said that she was one of those who lived by herself and that receiving my note helped her "get through each day." I humbly read numerous other replies of gratitude, and if ever I questioned the power of empathy and connecting deeply, or wondered about taking a chance at being personal, that moment, in this emerging crisis, convinced me.

Of course, I wrote this email from a position of power and privilege at BCG as the North America chair, but that position also comes with the added pressure of many years of formality, expectations, and rigor. Still, it afforded me the freedom to take big risks without fear of consequence. And that included the risk of trying to connect, deeply and personally, with everyone.

That experience, among others, led me to firmly believe that the generosity of real and humanized communication at work is a conduit for true collaboration. It sets a tone of positive energy and makes a generative environment

- where others feel seen and that they have a contribution;
- with a deep sense of trust among team members.

I, of course, cannot prove causality, but the comments from our North America team, to me and other leaders, made it clear that our employees felt heard (even if they did not always agree with the decisions) and connected both to BCG overall and to one another. BCG's performance, in one of the rockiest of times, also reinforced my belief that humanizing one's communications and building connections helps to drive business performance.

The outcomes of this generous communication become exponential. They lead to more effective overall team dynamics, enhance your own performance as a result of your understanding of others and your own impact, and lead to better overall business results.

THE CHALLENGE: BRINGING YOUR WHOLE SELF TO WORK

Many of us, for most of our working lives, are trained that deep, personal connections at work are inappropriate or even risky. We are taught that we must always remain professional in the workplace and leave the personal connections for the friends-and-family part of our lives.

That 45-minute exploration of my own feelings, before I sent the early-morning email, confirmed how I had been conditioned. I wondered,

- *What will other leaders think of me?*
- *Will I diminish my ability to be in charge?*
- *Who am I to know how all those employees are feeling?*
- *If I do take the chance, are the words I've chosen the right ones?*

While the right choice of words can contribute to a deeper connection, the wrong choice can push you backward. Similarly, the depth of connection is often influenced by the level of openness, authenticity, or humility and how those practices invite others to also respond openly, thereby contributing to a positive collaborative environment.

But while there's always some risk in making the wrong choice, one thing is certain: if we follow the conventional wisdom of the past and leave the personal connections at home, we end up trying to lead at work *with* work—data, numbers, clean lines of work-related subject matter. We wind up in one-dimensional relationships with all the three-dimensional human beings in our organizations. We leave parts of ourselves at home, and, in so doing, we lose the ability to understand others, to build relationships and trust that enable others to contribute and excel at their best. We might miss opportunities as an organization.

THE RESEARCH: CONNECTING INSPIRES

Not surprisingly, people want to feel connected to their leaders. A study by Brunswick Group of 5,000 employees noted that people prefer to work for a connected leader by five to one. They trust the connected leader far more than a detached leader. The study also noted that communicating with honesty and transparency is a key driver of employee motivation and retention.[1]

And the benefits of connecting personally with your teams go even deeper. A broad-based lack of connection has probably never been tested as deeply as it was during the pandemic. The 2021 *World Happiness Report* showed that people who experienced an increase in connectedness with others during the pandemic had greater life satisfaction, more resilience, and better mental health.[2] According to BetterUp research, the resilience fostered by connection led to 5 percent improved productivity—a stark contrast to the significant productivity declines seen by those less resilient.[3]

A Willis Towers Watson study showed that the greatest driver of employee engagement worldwide is if people feel their managers and organizations have genuine concern for their well-being.[4] To show that concern, you have to be visible; you have to connect. Connecting broadly, through heartfelt and intentional emotion, will go a long way toward inspiring and motivating your teams and employees.

HOW TO COMMUNICATE FOR DEEPER CONNECTIONS

You may believe you can't find the right words, the right tone, to connect deeply. You may not be sure of the techniques, tools, or methods you should use to begin to build connections without crushing your day—whether your team is just two people or thousands. The first step in figuring all this out involves taking time, a very rare commodity in our daily lives, and you must believe it's worth your time and investment to do the work.

See the Person, Not the Role

When you make time to connect with the *person*, and not just the person in their role, you make them feel seen. They are then more willing to connect openly with you. In other words, you build trust.

Joaquin Duato, chairman and CEO of Johnson & Johnson (J&J), has a long track record of, and great reputation for, connecting closely with his teams and his organization. Joaquin began his J&J career in 1989 in Spain, and it has spanned many roles. I asked Joaquin why he is able to connect so effectively. He explained,

> I think it starts with the fact that I simply like people. I am a pretty normal guy, quite casual, but I'm fortunate to have good empathy, EQ [emotional intelligence], and cultural awareness.
>
> Where did this come from? It began with my upbringing. I am from Spain, as you know. I had sixteen aunts and uncles and thirty-six first cousins. That family taught me to be flexible, to adapt, but also how to connect. Most importantly for me, the family also served as a backbone of stability, providing great strength from which I could draw.
>
> My dad was also very social. He instilled in me the value of caring, the importance of knowing the names of my colleagues, whatever their role and level in the organization. And not just their names but get to know them a bit as a person, not only as a role in the company. This encouragement to see others as more than their roles has served me well over the years. If I am trying to communicate something important to the teams, I really think about the listener, how will they hear it. This has enabled me to connect more effectively, and personally, with employees.

People make the difference. People get results. If you're describing a breakthrough made by one of your employees, do you say it was great to see what the *lead account payables rep* came up with? Or do you say, "Wow, it was great to see what James solved for us"? When you call James out as a person, connecting to him individually rather than to his role, you let him—and everyone else—know that you trust him and reinforce his engagement.

This applies in the team setting as well. When you're looking for creative ideas, or clever insights into a challenge, you can work to connect with everyone on your team. When you turn to people for their personal and collective experience, wisdom, and unique thinking, they will feel pride in their contributions and feel more confident offering additional insights in the future. As a result, you gain a richer set of information and achieve better problem-solving systems and more team cohesion.

Joaquin's dad's advice to see the person, not the role, when communicating strongly resonates with me. As I reflect on my BCG leadership experience, two examples vividly drive home the importance of seeing the person.

During the initial COVID-19 lockdown in 2020, while the benefits of working from home were often touted—time with children, reduced commute time, less travel, et cetera—it was not, of course, all roses. I met with one of our team members by Zoom. He was on his bed. I asked him why the bed. He told me he lived with his spouse in a small space. They traded off "desks"—one week she had the living room and he had the bed; then they swapped. This was a clear lesson that a consultant may be a consultant, but one's experience is sure not another's, and I would be wise not to forget it in my connections with my teams.

A second, emotional experience occurred when I joined one of our accessibility-network meetings. While this employee group initially focused on physical disabilities, it had evolved to encompass the growing impact of anxiety and other mental health issues. The group of hundreds started the session with one of the members sharing her battle with anxiety. It was moving.

Nearly all were in tears. It moved me. This was another powerful lesson of seeing a person. All of these BCG employees were individuals with their own singular opportunities and challenges to work through as they performed their roles. And the speaker, by sharing her unique experiences, drove home the idea that when leaders know their employees, they can work with them more thoughtfully and offer support that brings out their best.

Make It Personal and Real

How do you build a bond based on honesty and genuine concern for another person? While my experiences, of course, will not be yours, I am always on the lookout for an opportunity to build trust. As many of us learned how to work from home in 2020, my colleagues innovated all sorts of interesting workspaces, and I saw an opportunity to have a bit of fun, and connect across our community, in a very personal way. My goal for this email was to humanize and equalize all of us at our day-to-day level:

From: Davis, Joe

Sent: Thursday, April 9, 2020, 6:47 a.m.

To: All Staff

Subject: Sharing moments from home

Dear all,

As we continue to work remotely, many of you have shared pictures and stories of how you are adapting. I am sharing a few from my home to show how we are getting creative in where we work, and I hope they'll bring a smile to your face.

We are also finding moments of joy and levity in these difficult times, whether it be through our families, friends, pets, a good workout, or a home-cooked meal. We are all in this together; I hope everyone continues to reach out to each other on video, Slack, text, and phone to share ideas, catch up, and make new connections.

Yours,
Joe

A response came in from one of my colleagues a few hours later. She wanted to "check in" and let me know that the makeshift ironing-board desk and the cat (included in a photo attachment in my email) brought a smile to her face first thing in the morning. Then she signed off: "That's it. Obviously, nothing super important to say." When I shared her email with my team, we felt quite the opposite. Her note and closing sentence were powerful in how they reinforced the value of personal connections. They can inspire others, build community, and enhance connection among our fellow humans at work. All of these in turn build the strength of the organization.

Arne Sorenson was Marriott Corporation's CEO from 2012 until his untimely death in 2021 from pancreatic cancer. During his tenure, Arne grew Marriott through multiple successful acquisitions, started a home-rental business, and made many of the Marriott brands more relevant for younger travelers. Arne was well known and beloved, not only for his success as someone who delivered top- and bottom-line results but as a progressive leader, one who took a very people-centric approach to his leadership. This people-centric approach, seen as "humanizing," was exceptional because of the scale of the organization. He was celebrated for his talent and benevolence and revered as a leader and expert of the "humanity-meets-business crossroads."

Arne gave a now-famous address to over 80,000 Marriott global associates in April 2020. "A Message from Arne" was delivered when the company was beginning to grasp the gravity of the COVID-19 pandemic and also during the height of his chemo treatments.[5] According to *Forbes* magazine, Arne "lowered the shield" through his deep and personal connection with viewers: "He was candid, vulnerable, humble, emotional, and hopeful."[6]

On-screen alone, and in a suit with his tie slightly off center, Arne said it was "the most difficult video message we have ever pulled together." His use of "we" was a wonderful show of humbleness because he was *part of a team* that needed to come together, in the face of the pandemic, rather than simply a leader in a position of authority. He was also authentic, showing up as his true and vulnerable self, totally bald from the medical treatments he'd been undergoing and courageously showing his own emotional vulnerability under the circumstances.

Powerfully personal, authentic, and vulnerable: that was Arne. And it can be you, too, whether you're in front of a group of 2 to 3 colleagues, a team of 30 to 50 people, or an organization of thousands.

Keep It Simple and Honest

When you communicate with simple and honest messages, you establish credibility and trust. Whatever news you are bringing, keep in mind the listener: where they're coming from, how they will be affected, and how they will hear your message.

Joaquin described his belief in the power of bold simplicity:

I believe in simple messages. I also am willing to be bold. I believe deeply in telling it like it is—that is my motto. . . . I know this can be uncommon in the corporate world, with all the skepticism about what the leader is really saying, the perceived "true objectives" of the organization, so I believe it is very important to message simply, yet boldly, with honesty. When I first moved here, from Europe, as you can imagine I was a bit more brutal. I told it like it is, sometimes too directly. I had to evolve that, especially in the US. But I still believe it is critical to tell it like it is. I want to create an environment where people are comfortable being open with one another, sensitive, of course, but still open, honest, and frank.

You want people to hear you, to connect, to understand the situation and the expectations, clearly, without skepticism. With that clarity they can effectively move forward, on point, with minimal lost time. So do not muddle the message. And always be honest.

Arne demonstrated this in his video. He was approaching his eighth anniversary with the company as CEO, and he said he had never had a more difficult moment than that one, in which he was honestly describing the cutbacks that were going to be taken, the "temporary" hotel closures that were underway. "There is simply nothing worse than telling highly valued associates, people who are the very heart of the company, that their roles are being impacted by events completely outside of their control."

Few leaders like to give bad news. It is a rare leader who wants to admit they are facing a problem they may not be able to solve. As a leader the tendency is to try to paint the best possible picture. Arne did not take that path. The compassion and honesty were heartfelt, and, judging by all the feedback following the video, it was evident that, while his content was clearly bad news, his sincerity and openness were inspiring and motivating to the associates.

Be Responsive

Each of us wants to know we are heard, to know that others know we are there. A powerful yet simple way to build connections is to simply respond. Rich Lesser, former BCG CEO, described to me how he made this a practice: "I have always believed in the power of connecting, Joe, from back when I was leading small teams right up to my role as CEO. When people reached out, they heard back, whether by a simple email or a phone call. And it was not just a cursory reply; I gave real responses. I received so much appreciative feedback over the years. They appreciated my interest in them, but they also valued how I helped individuals 'clarify their thinking.'"

Use Tools to Your Advantage

When used well, video can be one of the most powerful tools for connecting with your colleagues. Even with a one-to-many ratio, a leader can connect deeply and personally through this technology.

Other effective communication tools are email, text and messaging apps such as Slack and WhatsApp, live team meetings, and even one-on-one sessions. As long as the delivery is clear, simple, honest, and heartfelt, each of these can create a powerful opportunity to connect.

You must communicate your points across multiple channels, multiple times, to move your team. For the most important communications, I have often found that a broad-based town hall or video message, backed by a broad-based email and supported with local live meetings reinforcing the message—with those in turn supported by local leadership emails—helps ensure that most hear the message in one venue or format or another. Frequency, when done well, matters.

CALL TO ACTION

Let me share four ideas to get you started on building the communication and connection muscles. These are techniques that have worked for many, including me. Remember, these are best if combined with care and honesty (which we will continue to discuss in future chapters).

Create a Sounding Board

I asked Joaquin what he does to help him connect personally and deeply with his organization. He prepares! He sets up sounding boards, which he calls *friend testing* and *group testing*, to get a sense of how his thoughts, concepts, messages, and even words will be heard and received when he presents them in larger venues. He also uses these trial runs to learn more about what is on his team members' minds and where they're feeling stress or uncertainty:

"Friend testing": I will often ask a business colleague, typically a friend who is deeper in the organization, who will tell me straight, what is landing, what is being heard. As I got into this role I asked a friend, *"What are they saying about me as CEO—what are they hearing as my message for J&J?"* He responded, *"Efficiency, need to tighten up, cut costs."* I noted I had never used those words or spoken to those points. I had been pushing simplification. He said, *"Yes, that is what you said, 'efficiency.'"* Big learning: one must test the message and the words over and over!

"Group testing": I use what I have come to call "listen and learns." They are typically small, eight-to-ten person sessions. I bring some of my latest thinking, testing my thoughts, ideas, messaging, and my word choice. I explain my ideas and ask folks to replay what I said. I often ask them to replay it to me as if they were telling their spouse or partner when they got home that night what they had heard from me that day. I listen for what words stuck in their minds, the words they use to explain what I said. In these sessions I will often use different words, literally, to see what sticks, to learn what gets lost in the mix. And then, of course, adjust my plans based on what resonates.

CALL TO ACTION

Identify and gather together a small group of business colleagues who will tell you straight. Practice your key messages on them before presenting to larger groups. Ask them what they heard and identify any disparities between your intended delivery and what messages were actually received.

Trim the Word Count

In my most recent role as BCG North America chair, I had a chief of staff who was also a dear friend and a great coach. Whenever I gave a speech, he would always come up to me afterward and point out all my asides, embellishments, fillers, and qualifiers. "All wasted words that greatly diminish your message and your impact," he said.

To this day, as I prepare a talk, I am constantly checking myself to be sure I am clear and concise, that I make the point fast. This also goes for written communications. A Gallup poll found that 70 percent of employees want shorter communications at work, which isn't surprising, given how reliant our society has become on short texts, tweets, and sound-bite podcasts. What may surprise you, however, is that a University of Maryland study reported that people only spend 26 seconds reading the things they choose to read, whether on social media, at school, or in the business setting.[7] I am not sure about you, but I now strive to write a note that can be read on one iPhone screen, no scrolling. And for years, my colleagues have teased me that I push them to use "48-point or so font" on PowerPoint (I was kidding), but the point is: fewer words.

CALL TO ACTION

As you prepare your speeches and written correspondence for the coming month, set a goal to trim the content by 15 to 30 percent.

Harness Technology

You are working in a world full of disruptions and new office-work models. When you harness more effective technology options, you maximize opportunities to get in front of, and connect with, people. Keep in mind the following:

- Teams notice when you are willing to commit to and leverage the platforms they prefer, whether it's email, Slack, text, Zoom, or any number of other options.
- People appreciate it when you use technology to reply promptly. Texting is quicker than email; email is quicker than snail mail. Of course, a timely reply doesn't always involve the latest software gadgetry. Sometimes it's quickest, and best, if you simply pick up the phone!
- Today's powerful video communication tools, such as Zoom, Teams, and Webex, promote better personal connections than nearly any written platform because they allow people to see facial expressions, hear vocal tones, and study body language.

CALL TO ACTION

Develop a three-prong plan to more effectively harness communication technology: identify your team's preferred platform, use rapid-response technology whenever possible, and rely on video technology for meetings whenever practicable.

Once, Twice, Three Times

For those messages we absolutely *must* land, the rule of three is the way to go. A good friend pointed out to me that a pair of Russian ice dancers, well known for their intricate footwork and choreography, always performed their sequences three times. The first time the judges saw it, they'd wonder, *What was that?* After the second time, the judges would think, *Wow, that's interesting.* And after the third pass, the sequence could be fully appreciated. The idea was that it would take three times for the beauty and talent of the performance to sink in.

This is what happens in the business world, too. You have to say something three times during your communications, especially if it is verbal versus written. The first time, the words will likely not fully sink in because your audience is also working to anticipate and interpret your full message. The second time, some of them may not hear you at all, as their minds drift back to the discussion with their child last night, or their phone call with their mom, or any other of life's intrusions. But after the third time, everyone will have had a chance to engage with what you said. This rule of three is particularly important in our information-saturated lives today. According to organizational psychologist Adam Grant, employees are exposed to 2.3 million words and numbers over a three-month period.[8] You try to keep that straight!

CALL TO ACTION

Whenever you prepare a presentation, whether for a regular team meeting or a speech to the entire organization, be sure to identify the overriding key message and then incorporate it three times into the body of your presentation. And, of course, spread it out: near the start, in the middle, and near the end.

FINAL THOUGHTS

A good, clear strategy is essential. A well-executed plan, with metrics and milestones, is critical. But these are not enough. You also want your team to bring their passion, their energy, their hearts to their work. That can be inspired by how you communicate. Being willing to share who you are, and show your heart, builds trust and loyalty. It also motivates others to collaborate and reveal the deeper challenges facing your team.

Connecting personally is essential, but a truly compassionate leader will go beyond communicating to connect. They will strive to listen and learn to truly understand *what they don't know*.

3

BE CURIOUS

Generous Listening

Generous leadership is about setting yourself aside to make room for the way someone else is thinking, to make room for the way they might see the world. It's an openness and an active setting-aside of our own experiences and beliefs to believe in another way of being, another person's way of seeing the world. Psychology books often call this *perspective taking* and define it as an ability to understand how a situation appears to another person *and* how that person is reacting cognitively and emotionally.

Of course, you can never fully understand another's experience, and claiming to, in fact, can be hurtful—this is a moment to bring self-awareness into the mix. "Oh, I understand where you are coming from" can be seen as an assumption. But you can *make the effort* to listen openly, and to try to hear another person's experience as they lived it. Consider that you don't know what you don't know. As you ask and try to understand another's point of view, be attuned to whatever information, facts, and insight they can offer that can be added to what you *do* know. Then that combined knowledge will afford you a better view into the option sets and a more deeply rooted understanding of the best possible paths forward.

A VIVID LEARNING EXPERIENCE

Steve Gunby and I were driving from DC to rural Pennsylvania to meet the CEO of a small regional retailer (you met Steve in an earlier chapter—he was my mentor and the first partner I worked for at BCG; he is currently president and CEO of FTI Consulting). As context, this company had been acquired by a larger retailer, our client, whom we had served for years. In short, we were the consultants to the acquiring company's CEO.

I was about to lead my first project and was excited about the opportunity. I knew I had a lot to learn, but in this moment, I was eager to head into that office and engage with a CEO! Not to show my stuff—that is not who I am—but to learn about him and his team as well as how we might help them. I had prepared extensively back in the office: created a nice PowerPoint presentation, practiced what I wanted to say, and even thought about how they might respond.

As we approached the beautiful small town, I eagerly started reminding Steve of all the things we were going to say—the prep about the company and the meeting we had done at the office. But as we pulled into the parking lot, he slowed me down.

"Look, Joe, you have good slides, and I know you are excited, but can we start from a different place here? Let's talk again about what we want to come out of the meeting and what we think *they* might want. What is the objective of this meeting?"

First, he asked me what I thought we wanted to happen at the meeting. *We have this covered*, I thought. Then he asked who I thought would be at the meeting. *Will it just be the CEO?* I had no idea who all he might have invited.

"What do we think *they* want from the meeting?"

I had not given this enough thought.

"How do you think *they* are feeling coming into this meeting? Who are we to them, and what do we represent?"

By now, I really didn't have any good answers to his questions. Although he thought we had the right materials for the meeting, he urged me to take a moment to think through how we were going to make this meeting useful for all.

We had discussed some of this back at the office, but I hadn't focused on it. Now, as he pushed me deeper and deeper and encouraged me to get as far into their heads as I could, I sat in that car, idling in the parking lot, feeling terribly naive. And also a little stupid and embarrassed. The drilling was tough, and I didn't have answers for Steve. But I got it—and I never forgot it!

Fortunately, Steve helped me engage, probe, and listen to their thinking and ideas from *their* perspective, to learn from them and respond to the anxiety that they were bringing into the room. But what a lost opportunity it would have been if we hadn't taken the time and emotional effort to think about the world from their perspective. As Steve put it to me years later when we were discussing this story, "You can't just come in with what you are going to say. You need to understand where they are coming from, *and* what they are going to hear."

It seems obvious to me now, after many years of practice, but putting yourself through the exercise my mentor put me through in that parking lot—thinking about the other person and preparing to engage them and listen to them—can have a lot of benefits beyond what might be quantified in numbers or dollars. Focusing on what you don't know

- shows deep respect for another person;
- puts people more at ease by giving them an opportunity to share;

- breaks down barriers of roles and titles;
- is a generous act of setting oneself aside to make room for another person's insight and experience.

The bulk of this chapter is focused on helping you understand how to do this incredibly important work. Treating people with respect and setting aside your own ego, opinions, and biases requires an incredible amount of courage and confidence. Doing this work is a true reflection of your humility and grace.

But it also is an opportunity for you to grow in important ways. Tactically, you learn from all the talent in the room, and you will be able to tap into better possible outcomes. As a leader you have an opportunity to understand the difference between what you are saying and what others may be hearing, shift your mindset to one of "we" versus "me," and show your willingness to learn. These generous acts are key to building a sustainable leadership practice in the ever-evolving workplace.

THE CHALLENGE: OPENING UP OUR MINDS

Why don't we work to better understand another's perspective? Sometimes it's a matter of not wanting to slow down and ask questions. Sometimes we aren't actively listening. And we are often stuck in our own minds, believing we know it all, believing we are right.

This point was viscerally driven home for me in a client meeting many years ago. The supply-chain vice president was presenting to the CEO in a conference room of his executive-suite peers. He was driving down a path in the presentation—his path—when the CEO, who I could see was listening intently and already thinking through the second-order implications of the ideas being presented, stopped him and asked a question that was orthogonal to the VP's storyline, a question they would all face if they followed the VP's recommendations. The presenter looked up, pondered the question briefly, and then—appearing not to have heard what was asked—essentially ignored the essence of the question (or did not stop long enough to understand it) and positioned his response right in line with the already planned flow of his presentation. It was fascinating to observe, and I will never forget what happened next: the CEO's eyes, after seeing that the VP had basically ignored his question, glazed over; he stopped listening and was disengaged for the rest of the presentation. The moment the VP chose to stay in his own head rather than trying to understand what was in the CEO's, he failed.

But the bigger obstacle in our data-driven, results-oriented world is that we don't think perspective taking (in particular, collecting views from many) has adequate value. We don't believe that it benefits the project outcome or the result—and we don't believe that it will ultimately benefit us, our career, or our future.

A very vivid example of this for me took place many years ago, when I had to outplace a senior manager from BCG. He was close to partner in tenure but not on track to make partner. He was an extremely bright, quick analyst and had good ideas, but they were his ideas—the ideas that came from his analysis. He did not truly engage with what others were thinking—and rarely, if ever, if they disagreed with him. I will never forget telling him his BCG career was over. He was a towering individual. He looked at me and, in tears, said, "What do you mean, I am not going to make partner?" I told him he simply did not listen; he was always stuck in his own head. He looked up. "But I don't get it; I listen!"

Even when we think there may be value and try to listen, we are often not motivated to put ourselves in someone else's shoes, to learn what they know that we may not, because we're too pressed for time or busy working toward a linear solution. We know it is all about the numbers. We think we have all the best information. But do we really?

THE RESEARCH

Two notable studies reveal the important traits and skills possessed by effective managers.

Asking Is Better than Telling

Google conducted a research study called Project Oxygen to determine what made its most effective managers great.[1] After surveying over 80,000 managers, it identified 10 traits that were common among its best. The number one trait? Being a good coach. And Google found that its best coaches understood that the way to engage and empower employees is to *ask and listen.*

According to the Google study, asking is more powerful than telling. When leaders talk and tell (or, to put it another way, control and command), employees learn to feel helpless and dependent. Morale and performance suffer. Conversely, asking for input

- engages the brain as people work to develop appropriate responses;
- encourages initiative as employees feel trusted and empowered;
- surfaces greater insights because engaged employees are actively growing, developing, and learning and are therefore better equipped to innovate;
- promotes connections because questions open the door for dialogue and create opportunities for employees to feel heard and respected.

Take Another's Perspective to Stimulate the Brain

How can we build critical problem-solving capabilities into our organizations?

Wharton marketing professor and neuroscientist Michael Platt and his coauthors, as part of the 2018 Wharton Neuroscience Initiative with leading Swedish corporate bank SEB, noted that one key strategy for building these capabilities may be taking the perspectives of others.[2] Not only does this crucial skill provide us with additional information about complex situations, it also activates brain regions linked with creativity and innovation. According to the study, the ability to solve problems and make decisions improved, as did inclusion, cross-collaboration, and risk management.

There is much research on the brain networks—the "mentalizing network" and the "exploration network"—that activate when we take the perspective of another person. When these two brain networks get going, Platt and his colleagues note, they boost activity that "provokes selection of options we typically wouldn't take into consideration" and "might allow us to come up with better ideas and hence make better decisions."

HOW TO LISTEN TO LEARN

Developing the ability to listen to learn, and the converse learning to listen, will be a critical differentiator in how you develop in your career, particularly in disruptive moments.

This was driven home for me during the difficult first year of the pandemic. I knew we were all struggling from not seeing others in person or receiving the typical on-the-job human immersion and learning. Debbie Lovich, a leader in BCG's People and Organization Practice, sent me an email asking me to speak with her about our staff's situation. The context was how far we should go in supporting our staff financially, beyond their normal paychecks; the specific issue was how much we should pay our people to equip their homes with what they needed to do their jobs and to reimburse them for food and other expenses. My initial reaction was that we paid people enough and they should be able to afford to pay for whatever they needed. And then I admitted my discomfort: "I truly do not get the problem; help me understand."

"Joe," she said. "Their reality is not yours. Their stress is huge, and the symbolism of an additional payment shows the love and care we have for our people, which extends well above the actual cost—although many appreciate the cost, too."

She reminded me that my circumstances were different from my staff's on multiple levels: Their living spaces. The reality that many employees had moved to new cities for their jobs and had yet to see an office or meet anyone live, face-to-face. Their technology needs. The complexities of creating home meals or having to rely on Uber Eats. The burdens of having to adapt to homeschooling for their children. Abrupt cancellation of all their typical social engagements. She pushed me to slow down, to take the time to meet virtually with many BCGers facing varied circumstances, and to work to understand what they were facing. I had to take the time to open my eyes and make space for these people's experiences, which were very different from my own. Only then could I adjust many BCG North America policies to appropriately react to accommodate my staff's lived experience.

The time and attention paid during those mostly Zoom calls, and the subsequent actions, were a sign of deep respect for the participants. Those conversations broke down barriers because they transcended roles in the organization and became about two people and a shared experience. The people on the other end of the video felt supported by the actions taken in response to what they shared.

What does perspective taking, and working to uncover what you do not know, look like in action? How can you implement this practice? Listen to some successful and experienced leaders break down the ways they have found to be better at their work through the lens of others.

Be Prepared and Do the Deep Thinking

First off, do not assume you know what others might bring to a meeting or conversation. Avoid mentally putting them in the box in which you typically see them. Instead, think in advance about the circumstances and the players, and consider their roles, but remain open to whatever their points of view may be. "Work hard in advance to connect to their mental map; invest the time and effort to try to understand how they are thinking about the world," as Steve Gunby put it to me. Then prepare a set of questions to invite their participation and perspectives.

This is the type of drilling my mentor put me through for the Pennsylvania retail meeting. Years later, I asked Steve for his thoughts about the importance of preparing for meetings and critical conversations. He said he'd push himself, and his teams, to deepen their knowledge as much as possible. Really think and understand what others might be thinking, what they might already know, why they are doing the things they are doing today, why others should care about your point of view and your ideas, what you are bringing that is value-added, or why a plan might not work for other people. Think about these in advance, and then give others the respect of valuing their time and knowledge. He told me this story:

> I had a client and mentor who drove home this lesson for me. I met with him over several meetings. The first meeting I prepared a thorough two-hundred-page deck. He looked at me and asked me,

"Why did you bring me a two-hundred-page deck, where is the meat, can't we just focus on the critical issues?!" So, the next meeting I brought a tight seven-page summary deck; guess what, he asked me again, "Where is the meat?! This is so high-level; can't we have a presentation that focuses on the critical issues?" The third time, I brought a different summary deck—one that high-spotted where we thought our findings were radically different than expected. I started off by saying, "[Client], we looked at the issues. I believe you started out with seven key thoughts on why this is working out as it is; five we have verified, but two are fundamentally different. I am happy to cover all seven, but my guess is you would rather focus on the two?" My client lit up and said, "Ah, great, finally we are having a meeting that gets to the meat!" and proceeded to drill into great detail on the two key areas that were new and different to him. To do this I had to spend the time to get into his head and understand what he already knew and believed so I could focus on what was different and therefore valuable for him. I had to care enough to prepare, to listen, to probe. You must reach out, hear them, understand. When you focus on *their* experience, it is going to be a win-win. You will enhance your credibility, of course, but it is also about really caring. This is not just a story for business; this is a story for life.

As I am preparing a presentation for a meeting with a client, whether alone or with my team, I now always find myself writing, reviewing, and saying each word on the page with my audience in mind. *How will they read that word? What is on their mind that will be activated by that sentence?* It has become second nature, but it took years of getting it and practicing it. I will say that I am still less good in my personal life.

Ask Thoughtful Questions

Listening to learn means asking thoughtful questions, and when you do this, you're modeling a good work ethic, humility, curiosity, and acumen. Ask "Why?": Why do they see something the way they do? What is their experience that informs their thinking? When you are interested, you draw others out, especially when you make sure you give others ample opportunity to share their perspectives. As you do this, you will deepen your knowledge.

When Joaquin Duato was a young manager, he managed sales reps who were much older than him—in their 50s. He described this as "tricky," and he approached the challenge by listening a lot and working hard to not be seen as a rival. He was there to learn, and he constantly asked the veteran reps for advice. "I learned a lot, and it was good for building connections," he said.

Tom Monahan, CEO of DeVry University, former executive chairman of ProKarma, and former chairman and CEO of CEB, also believed in the importance of asking thoughtful questions. He wanted to make sure he fully understood what others were truly thinking. He observed that it's "rarely obvious what to do" when making big decisions. He noted, "You need to see the entire picture before you make a call. That's why I like to ask a lot of questions. I am always looking for great questions, stealing good questions, curating great questions." He also urged trying to understand where other people's questions are coming from: "When people ask something of *me*, I think it is also critical to really understand the question. By that I mean: What does the questioner really want to know? How are they thinking about their question? For example, I always find it interesting when someone asks about our performance. I reply by asking what metrics they're using. With that knowledge, I can fully answer the question without guessing about how to interpret their query."

Tom was asked to give some advice a while back that illustrated the importance of asking questions and getting multiple perspectives. About a decade ago, when leaders were just beginning to work at creating truly diverse and inclusive workplaces, one of Tom's colleagues was in the process of a gender-affirming transition, and they asked him when they should switch bathrooms. He bounced that one around in his head, not quite sure how to answer. So he asked around, and he collected some great answers and some snarky answers. One person suggested his colleague should switch bathrooms when it felt most comfortable for them to do so. This was enlightening: "I realized I was asking the wrong question—I was asking colleagues about what would make *them* comfortable. The right question, and the one I should have asked, was what would make the colleague who was transitioning most comfortable."

Listen Carefully

Once you've done the work of preparing and then asking excellent questions, listening carefully becomes the next critical step. Your goal is to understand the content of the meeting or discussion from the other person's perspective, in their context, and to apply what you learn from them—including a richer set of insights and data—as you move forward with evaluating what actions you might take.

Scott Kirby has been a lifelong airline person, and he took over the reins as CEO of United Airlines just as his industry and the globe were being rocked by the pandemic in May 2020. These challenges enabled him to stretch his standard leadership capabilities, his strong desire to connect with his employees, and his belief in the importance of listening:

I speak face-to-face with every person who is to be promoted to a managing director position in United and have done three to four hundred interviews. I recently spoke with three candidates, each of whom had started as United technicians (mechanics) more than thirty years earlier. Technicians are one of the hardest groups for me to connect with. They are not in the front lines facing customers; they are off in the hangars. Anytime they do interact with the customer, it's negative, as they are only on the airplane when something may be broken. When I asked each of them what technicians most care about and what was their number one complaint, the answer from all three was unanimous: We don't have enough spare parts.

What an epiphany! Our technicians want to do their job well. What creates pride for them is fixing the airplane—a great testament to how much they care about the company. But when the company lets them down by not having enough spare parts, they feel a lack of pride. Even if the parts inventory was initially set at the right level according to the spreadsheet math, when something goes wrong and there aren't enough parts, pride becomes undermined. And eventually, whether subconsciously or consciously, they'll wonder: *If the company doesn't care, why should I care?* Since then, I've started saying, "The spreadsheet is not necessarily 'fact.' It is a starting point, but the world is messier than the spreadsheet, and it cannot account for the pride of the brand and the impact of whatever decision we're making."

I had the chance to listen and learn, and I recognized that going past whatever the spreadsheet says is a culture change. The finance team may be averse, when they look at the budget for the next year and want to say "no" to the extra parts. But I trust that supporting the pride in our technicians is going to pay bigger dividends. Those little things—you can't put in your spreadsheets, but you can see the results.

I now have a straightforward philosophy. I learn more about what's going on at United when I ask questions. Once you get people talking, they trust you more. If you're genuinely listening to their views—even if you don't always agree with them—you learn something.

Rich Lesser also cited the importance of building teams who would challenge him: "Whether it was my early days of leading a client team, running an office, or as CEO, I gravitated to people who were going to challenge me. I was always probing to get to the best answer, to find the highest-quality ideas. I wanted to get to the truth."

None of the CEOs I spoke with have an "I know it all" attitude. Tom says it's important to question deeply before you leap to an answer, so you can learn and respond thoughtfully, with true interest and noble intent. Scott values the importance of making bold, counterintuitive decisions. Rich surrounds himself with people who are going to challenge him. Joanne Crevoiserat, CEO of Tapestry, loves to hear from the *least* tenured in the room. As she put it to me, "Always strive to learn, and seek to understand, what you do not know. Be approachable so that others are comfortable engaging and providing their perspective. I always look for the views of the less-tenured people in the room and gain a lot of insight from their perspective."

Each CEO described it in their own way, based on their individual experiences, but their behaviors are consistent: rather than operating in accordance with hierarchy, they listen because they know each person knows something they do not know and can offer input that can surprise them, give them pause, make them ponder from new angles, and ultimately enable them to make better decisions.

CALL TO ACTION

For many of us, running a meeting, or meeting with and probing others one-on-one, is second nature, and no one should have to tell us how to do it. On the other hand, we sometimes know our jobs, and the content, so well—and we are so experienced in what we do—that we don't see where we can make improvements. Engaging with others on autopilot might have been fine under the old-fashioned leadership model, but no more. If you're trying to become more effective, really learn from others, and inspire others to be full contributors, you have to change. Here are some steps you can take to get started.

(Over)prepare for Meetings

Because we have a lot of experience running meetings, we are often tempted to resist spending much time planning our meetings or engagements. We skip thinking deeply about the meeting or the participants or how to achieve the best value with the time. We are certain we can just wing it. But that isn't always in the best interests of our people. And it does not show respect.

I can think of so many times I created an agenda well in advance, reviewed it as I walked in the door, and just got at it. Worked just fine when it was my leadership team! But I can recall the sting of meetings when it was not just my team but a broader collection of colleagues by whom I was rightly caught off guard when they conveyed what was on their minds and I would find myself scrambling to respond effectively.

CALL TO ACTION

Before going into a group meeting, do your own "state-of-mind" prep and ask yourself a thorough set of questions, for 5 to 15 minutes, considering the following:

- Whom are you meeting?
- What is the knowledge and experience they are bringing into the room?
- What is their connection to the topic and to you?
- What beliefs are they bringing into the room that might be in contrast to yours?
- What do you know about what is on their mind, if only in an organizational context?
- What might be their motives and intentions?
- What do you think is their emotional state, especially compared with (or in contrast to) yours?
- What new ideas might they bring to the group's knowledge base? To your personal knowledge base?
- Are you ready to be surprised with insights you didn't expect?
- Are you ready to better engage with others and to accept their perspectives?

Ask Questions

Christina Sistrunk, the former CEO of oil- and gas-production company Aera Energy, shared some thoughts about what she called "skillful engagement": "Take others' points of view into account as much as you can, at every stage of your career journey—particularly from those you do not know. By this I mean get behind the why with people, not just the what. Work to put others at ease so you can listen and learn. When you create relationships that enable others to give you their true perspective, you can generate real value with those insights. Be sure to probe others. What they know, what they have experienced, why."

Of course, to implement her suggestions, you need to ask thoughtful (and not demanding) questions.

CALL TO ACTION

Let me suggest that, for important one-on-ones, you set aside time to ask people for their perspectives, just as I have suggested you do in preparing for and running a group meeting.

- What are they experiencing related to the topic at hand?
- What do they see as the challenges or opportunities of the relevant topic?
- Why do they see things the way they do?

Listen for their insights that are new to you, or not as you expected or believed, and probe deeper on those. Share your views and get their thoughts on your perspectives. Quickly run yourself through the same set of questions I have suggested for a group meeting.

If you practice doing this often, it will become second nature every time you meet with others.

Engage the Skeptics

Have you ever been in a room, presenting an idea for change, and someone says, "Oh, that will never work"? Or you've solicited feedback as you work through your options, and you hear the "No, we cannot do that"? Your instinct might be to be defensive or just ignore them, but their perspective and experience, if you can embrace it, will strengthen your position. Asking for *more* information about why they feel the way they do, and then listening carefully to what they say, can be the best course of action. One BCG colleague recounted a story that illustrates the necessity of this process:

> We were helping a company determine if they should move one of their operating sites. They were considering a lower-cost location in a different part of the country, and the BCG project manager had completed a very detailed cost analysis. He presented a very thorough look at the pros and cons. Along the way, the company president stopped him and said, "This analysis is all great, but what about the diversity challenge? We know this is an expensive location, but it is our site with the most diverse group of managers, and if we move, we lose so many important people. How are you solving for that?"
>
> The room became silent, the BCG team dumbfounded. After the client representatives left the room, the BCG senior team member turned to the project leader. "What the heck?!"
>
> "What do you expect, for me to be an EEOC [Equal Employment Opportunity Commission] expert?" the project manager responded.
>
> "No, I expected you to bicycle your solution around the organization and ask what is wrong with it. Do you think someone in the HR department didn't know there was an EEOC issue?"
>
> Although the BCG project leader had done exceptional analysis, he had lacked the humility in this case to realize he may not know everything, expand his research, and prepare for the naysayers.

CALL TO ACTION

As you are seeking a solution to a problem in your work, be sure to find those most likely to be skeptical of your idea and find out why, really. When someone tells you it will not work, do not assume they are a blocker; rather, deeply probe as to why, and solve their *nos*. Similarly, as you prepare your meeting agendas, plan to specifically ask for input from those who disagree with you so you can learn from the "no-ologists" in the room. As uncomfortable as this might be, these sorts of questions—and ensuing discussions—can sometimes prompt decidedly innovative ideas.

Seek Perspectives across Your Organization

I do not care what your level is, or what the size of your organization is, or how much information you think you control—you do *not* know it all. Reaching out and learning *across the organization* can be so powerful because, when you endeavor to seek other perspectives, you can tap into the pulse of your organization, learn about another department, understand the latest trends of the new generations, and create community. But of course, meetings held in giant auditoriums are often not the right settings for people to feel safe enough to open up. Whether it be Joaquin's group or friend testing, find your tools and methods to reach out, listen, and learn.

CALL TO ACTION

Reflect on some of the venues where you have engaged in meaningful conversations beyond the workplace with family and friends. What made those settings effective? What was it about the structure, content, or flow of the discussions that prompted open participation? Drawing on some of these positive experiences, create your own version of kitchen-table discussions to provide that safe, open space for your people to speak up and help you learn what you need to learn.

FINAL THOUGHTS

I strive, in every interaction, to ensure that I am seeing the issue, the discussion, that moment, from the perspective of others. What is on their mind? What is their situation? What is their relevant background to this topic? Why might they feel the way they do when I feel differently? Why are they drawing a particular conclusion when I am drawing a different one? What can I learn from their perspective? What do they know that I do not? What is the best path when I combine our perspectives?

You never know when the practice of perspective taking might have a profound impact. I was powerfully reminded of this, or better schooled on the importance of trying, at my alma mater during a Whitman College Board of Trustees meeting.

The student-body president, a graduating senior, was meeting with the board for the final time. She gave a powerful speech, with such passion and vulnerable emotion from the heart that she choked up as she admonished us to work hard to try to relate to another's lived experience—to *not* sit in our "ivory tower" seeing the world through our predominantly white, privileged lenses.[3] She asked us to *listen* to her: the first Latina first-generation daughter of undocumented parents to serve as Whitman College student-body president. And to listen to all the others like her. To realize our situation was not hers, and hers today will not be that of the students of 3, 5, and 10 years from now. She told us to look forward, taking the perspective of the next generation of incoming students, to ensure the viability of the college we all love so much.

I imagine this accomplished young woman was feeling a swell of many emotions: nostalgia, pride, maybe some trepidation for the future. But she also felt a sense of urgency in her message to us, this audience of affluent individuals, enough to issue a challenge to commit to this practice of empathy and making space and openness. Do these practices allow you to work more collaboratively with your teams, broaden your circle, and open channels further to learn even more? Yes, they do. And when you seek to get the best possible information in these ways, and broaden the group of people you are asking, you give more people a seat at the table!

4

WELCOME EVERYONE

Generous Inclusion

When you have an opportunity to bring others into a conversation, you are inviting collaboration. You are recognizing the value of another's contributions.

In this case I mean all voices. Those at more junior levels who have relevant expertise, those in different parts of the organization who have perspectives unique to your team, and those from diverse backgrounds and life experiences who are often left out and will bring a richness to the thinking.

This practice can happen at any leadership level. It's less about hierarchy and more about valuing input. When included for their expertise and unique point of view, people are inspired; they feel more personally empowered, more valued. You build goodwill. These more inclusive teams can get more done and do their job better.

But first *you* must act—it is on *you* to make it possible for people to be in the room. Whether you are a sales rep early in your career or a more senior leader, you want the lines of communication to be open with your team, and empathy is the way to accomplish this.

During the second lockdown, I regularly worked to get a read on our staff's wider lens with a technique I called "kitchen tables." The name comes from the blue kitchen table in our home. Our family, with four children, seven years from oldest to youngest, gathered at this table for meals and opened and fast-paced conversations. It was sometimes stressful and always animated, and even though we often had spirited disagreements, there was a lot of learning. At BCG, I organized Zoom calls for 5 to 25 people from the more junior cohorts. I asked how they were feeling, their sense of how others were feeling, what they believed were the key flash points, where they thought BCG was off, and where I was off. I worked very hard to listen and learn.

And I learned much during those sessions. I recall one powerful moment when the group mentioned to me that I should be more inclusive in my broader BCG communications, town halls, or emails. By this they did not necessarily mean that I should be more inclusive of any one group but that I should be more inclusive of all; in this instance, they meant BCG's different business units, in particular those acquired by BCG. But the point was clear: ensure my communications are fully inclusive. A bit stunning for a person who takes pride in building inclusivity!

The burden is on you to ensure your tables are inclusive, which means you may need to expand your mindset, humility, confidence, and patience; this is the mindset of a generous leader. You will have to be the one who ensures those opportunities for inclusion exist, and you will have to be the one who consciously creates them, not only with your scheduled agenda but also with your encouragement, your questions, and your active listening.

And then, of course, it is your subsequent action that really matters—and that's what this chapter is about. Not only that you invite people into the room, but that they are heard and valued and that they understand they are essential to a successful result. How you behave and what you signal will make or break the level, and effectiveness, of inclusivity at your tables.

FRONTLINE INSPIRATION

Christina Sistrunk shared with me an excellent example of the power of inclusion—the benefits of bringing many to the table. She had worked to make safety a priority during her time at Shell EPW, and when, after great progress, she noticed improvements had plateaued, she leveraged an idea she'd learned from one of the company's contractors: a twice-per-year field-team meeting on safety.

> I invited in three hundred of our field supervisors (both company and contractors) to discuss safety and what they could do to make our track record even better. The design was a two-day, everybody-at-the-table meeting. As we were planning the meeting, the field group asked if they could hold the first day's meeting by themselves—no managers, no brass. This was very unusual in the Shell culture. But I agreed. I had to show them I cared; I had to allow others to step up and open up. To be together, engage, talk, and work to generate their own set of ideas. I needed to flex our typical top-down corporate command model to get results.
>
> On the second day, we brought in the full team to listen—the field supervisors and my management team. We opened the meeting with a powerful guest speaker, an oil-field worker who told his story of taking small safety shortcuts and the resultant impact, on himself and his family, which was brought about by life-changing injuries. Everyone in the room was deeply moved.
>
> I then continued the conversation with twenty-four human silhouettes up on the stage. I pointed out those that represented

people who were injured during the previous year. I then, during a break, multiplied those silhouettes by four and pointed out these were the families and friends also affected by the injury. This moved us into a very productive discussion for the balance of the day where a lot of ideas—and solutions—were shared. Our leaders were willing to do more for their loved ones than they would do even for their own safety.

This problem-solving structure, moving from a corporate compliance approach to a shared-solutioning approach, was groundbreaking for my department. It was an important signal that management cared and that we recognized not only them, but their families—it was a signal that *I* cared to build a company culture of engagement and, in this case, one where safety was always paramount.

The benefits were inclusion, ownership, and gaining commitment and alignment. The field-leadership group felt more empowered and aligned, and they demonstrated how they cared for their people instead of relying solely on rules and procedures to keep people safe.

When we brought the people together that the workers saw as their leaders—both company and contractors without the supervisors' bosses, we had "one of their own" facilitate a real discussion about improving safety. They unpacked excuses and learned for themselves that they got to choose how much time they spent leading their people with accountability versus accomplishing an enormous list of tasks (answering emails, calls from engineers, et cetera). Part of this was getting them to see with fresh eyes how much the people working for them needed them and also to believe that leadership would stand behind them if they asked for what they needed. We couldn't tell them this in a presentation; they had to explore the barriers, examine their choices, and have the space to make commitments to lead differently. They made those commitments. Ultimately, that team delivered a 60 percent reduction in injuries year-on-year for more than two years running.

In this example, the inclusion of a diverse working group created a unique and unprecedented collaboration within the organization. It also created intimacy and connection where before there was none, and this intimacy, especially in a traditionally unfeeling industry, was special and incredibly fertile.

Here's a smaller-scale but personally influential example from my own experience. Connor Kennel, a finance analyst at BCG, told me how bringing him into the room and including him in our discussions had been personally motivating and empowering:

> I was a new finance analyst at BCG, in my early twenties. I was the number cruncher, responsible for analyzing a sliver of the business. Usually it was crank the numbers, fill out the report, send it along. But you made a real difference for me. When you had meetings with finance, you invited us—the least tenured analysts—into the room or onto the conference call. You always acknowledged each of us, and if the conversation turned to our numbers, you asked us questions. It was uncomfortable at times, being probed, when you are used to simply emailing a report. But it was also exhilarating. It was empowering. It drove me to want to understand more deeply how my pieces fit in, and it inspired me to want to help even further if, and when, I could.

Needless to say, Connor is a talented individual. He has since been promoted at BCG and has been invited to work in an international office, sharing his knowledge of US operations and expanding his own knowledge and capability set. But this experience of being recognized for his contributions was still meaningful for Connor. He thought his work was insignificant. He thought he was insignificant. And here was a senior-level manager drawing attention to his excellent work product, showcasing his contribution to the project.

When you invite others into the room and encourage them to actively work together and fully participate with their unique knowledge base and experience, it is a generous act toward that person because

- you show that you recognize them and value them;
- you give them room to have a voice;
- you encourage and support them.

But these acts are also generative in the way described earlier as "contributions to something bigger." This kind of inclusion encourages individuals to think collectively about the direction of the organization, beyond just *their* role and space, into broader possibilities. Welcoming voices at the individual level can also help people evolve from being simple "doers" to being active participants. Finally, it ultimately yields better outcomes for an organization when employees at all levels feel empowered and motivated to work beyond the scope of their role.

THE CHALLENGE: IDENTIFYING BLIND SPOTS

Many corporate cultures are like the one described by Christina, where a top-down approach to solving problems is taken rather than inviting the frontline employees to participate. I recall in my own early leadership days being given some grief for connecting to people "so low" in the organization. Some leaders also find it's just faster and easier for them to come up with the solutions and tell everyone what to do. But that doesn't always lead to the best decisions.

The blind spots and other sources of resistance that leaders tend to struggle with, when thinking about including more people at the table, include the following:

- linear thinking about roles and hierarchy;
- insecurity about being challenged in a room where you are leading a meeting;
- lack of certainty on how to effectively include and engage those not typically in your meetings;
- reluctance to potentially introduce chaos;
- hiding behind the excuse of "inefficiency."

When I decided to begin inviting people to the table, it started out as selfishly practical. By going straight to those on the front line, I actually got answers faster than I would have waiting for information to move down and up the channels. I could ask real-time questions, and I got the straight scoop. It took me some time, but I eventually also realized that I wasn't the only one benefiting, and I decided to build this into my leadership skill set.

THE RESEARCH: THE MANY BENEFITS OF BEING INCLUDED

Surveys show that today's employees want to feel connected. This became especially true as the world came out of the challenges of working remotely for nearly two years during the beginning of the pandemic, but experts expect this trend to continue. The significance of this is quite clear: when employees feel included, they are more likely to fulfill their potential. And when this is the case, you and your organization are more likely to deliver your expected business results.

BCG created a new index for measuring inclusion after surveying 27,000 employees across industries in 16 countries. The Bias-Free, Leadership, Inclusion, Safety, and Support (BLISS) Index found that employees who feel happiness and empowerment at work are better able to fulfill their potential by 30 percentage points over those employees who feel less satisfied.[1]

In terms of inclusion, authenticity was highly correlated with it. When people felt they could bring their full self into the workplace and believed their perspective mattered, they engaged more openly and were 2.4 times less likely to quit. Also, the behaviors and diversity modeled by the top-line leaders, as well as the direct-line leaders, were critical to successfully building a feeling of inclusion among the teams. When the leaders created an environment where it felt safe to speak up, make mistakes, and take risks without fear of reprisal, 80 percent of employees felt their perspectives mattered. In contrast, this statistic dropped to just 30 percent in organizations where staff didn't feel safe to fully contribute. Similarly, at organizations that promoted employee participation, only 4 percent of employees self-identified as an attrition risk (indicating they are not likely to stay with their current company), compared with organizations where employees didn't feel supported, where 17 percent of employees self-identified as considering leaving.

In his book *10 Leadership Virtues for Disruptive Times: Coaching Your Team through Immense Change and Challenge*, Tom Ziglar cites Google's Project Aristotle, which found that the most effective teams practice inclusivity, respect, and participation.[2] Inclusivity means including everyone who needs to be there, allowing multiple communication styles—talking, texting, sharing documents, and so forth—and ensuring everyone knows the meeting's agenda. Respect means welcoming all team members and ensuring everyone feels safe. Participation means everyone contributes. The project also noted some simple actions that show respect, appreciation, and recognition, actions that build inspiration:

- start each meeting by spending 5 to 10 minutes recognizing and showing appreciation for specific team members;
- offer inspiration by sharing quotes and stories;
- end each session by recognizing and giving specific praise for people's meeting contributions.

The study found, not surprisingly, that leaders showing respect for and actively including participants contribute to an atmosphere where collaboration and innovation flourish.

In her book *Which Two Heads Are Better than One? How Diverse Teams Create Breakthrough Ideas and Make Smarter Decisions*, Juliet Bourke describes how her research showed the benefit of bringing many to the table to capture the full diversity of thinking.[3] Through this wellspring of creativity, innovation is enhanced by about 20 percent while risks are reduced by up to 30 percent.

HOW TO EMPOWER BY INCLUDING

Inclusion can take many shapes and sizes. You might set up a short-term group formed to work for just a couple of days to attack a mutual problem. You might establish regular update meetings within parts of your organization (finance, HR, et cetera) where you invite employees who typically do the unseen prep work. You might create sounding boards, such as my kitchen table or Joaquin's friend-testing groups, formed to gather further insight into your organization and offer valuable input into your thinking. You might leverage your diversity networks (employee resource groups in many organizations) beyond the role of supporting their specific affinity groups and include them more deeply in business challenges and opportunities. Or you might simply expand your regular management meetings to a broader group to benefit from more voices, more experiences, and more wisdom. If you stop to give it some thought, you'll likely see that, in any given week, there are many opportunities to invite additional perspectives and ideas.

Recognize Value

Everyone you work with wants to contribute, to make a difference. They want to know they are a valued team member, and they want to be part of the team's performance. That means your invitation must be offered with genuine intention. And once they're in the room, you must listen to them, seek to uncover what *they* know, and keep them motivated to participate.

Susan Grimbilas, head of HR for BCG globally, shared one of her personal experiences about being recognized:

> Many years ago, I worked in a health-insurance company. I worked for a selfish manager; it was all about him. He might call you into a meeting, but there were rules. You had to arrive before he did. You had to have a standard leather portfolio and a Cross pen for note-taking. I am not sure he ever heard a word anyone said at *his* tables. It was very clear to me he cared only about himself.
>
> I contrast this with sitting at BCG North America management tables. During one of our meetings, unfortunately—as too often happens to the women in the room—I was being talked over. Then I made a statement about some topic and received no reaction. Another person in the room—yes, a man—repeated my

statement, and an entire conversation ensued. I was very moved at what happened next. One of the male leaders in the meeting grabbed the floor, stopped the discussion, and asked if anyone else observed what had just happened to me. It was a very powerful moment of feeling included.

The issue for Susan was that her idea had value, but it wasn't recognized as such when she, a woman, presented it. When one of her colleagues stopped the meeting to be sure everyone understood what had happened, she, and her idea, was recognized and validated.

When we think of inclusion, we think of inviting people at lower levels of the organization who might not otherwise have the opportunity to participate. But sometimes people at higher levels are also left out, whether because their field of expertise might not be recognized as relevant or for other reasons—which can unfortunately be tied to gender identity, race, ethnicity, and so on. Geraldine Rhodes, a BCG manager at the time of COVID-19, shared how honored she was when she was tapped to be part of the company's COVID response team: "I still remember when I got the phone call from the head of our Northeast system to join BCG's COVID response team in March of 2020. It went something like this: 'Geraldine, can you be in Philly today? We have a problem with COVID, we might have to shut the offices. We need you up here. Can you help?' It was one of the most meaningful moments in my career, to be included, and an opportunity to stretch, learn, and lead in new ways."

Highlight Expertise

People love to be at the table. It is motivating and inspiring, even if at times it can be scary. Highlighting someone's expertise, when delegating a task, is a generous way to surrender control and invite others into problem-solving.

Joanne Crevoiserat shared with me a story from her time at the retailer Kohl's where she leveraged expertise to the benefit of both parties:

> I thought I was in line for, and wanted, the CFO job at Kohl's, but our CEO asked me to be the EVP, merchandise planning. He wanted someone with a financial background in the role who also knew some merchandising . . . like me.
>
> I had never done the formal merchandise-planning role, and here I was with six SVPs, all deep in their roles; I did not know this job. I really had to learn to use, and rely on, my team. A key competitor went out of business in advance of the back-to-school season, and we needed to take advantage of this huge opportunity. I included each leader in the target-setting and planning, sorted out who had which expertise for this moment, we assigned roles and goals, and then I let the team run. They did a great job.
>
> By including them in this first big opportunity and leveraging their capabilities, we achieved our targets. More importantly, they immediately felt this new leader (me) would include the team. Of course, I made some mistakes along the way, but this first experience taught me that humility is a huge leadership skill and asset.

Joanne knew that she couldn't do it all on her own and had to actively include the experience of her team.

John Rice is CEO of Management Leadership for Tomorrow (MLT). MLT equips and emboldens high-achieving individuals from underrepresented communities—Black, Latinx, and Native American—to realize their full potential, to make a mark, to make a difference. John went from college to AT&T, then Disney, then the NBA, before founding MLT. He had a similar story, describing the importance of leaning on his team's expertise to ensure the group's success:

When I was working for the NBA, I had a big transition when I took the job of building the Japan business. At the time, it was the NBA's largest international market. I realized that, for the first time in my career, there was no one more senior in the organization who knew that market well enough to help guide the success. We were on our own in Japan. There was a team already on the ground but given I spoke no Japanese, and they had varying levels of English, I had to work hard to communicate. I had to quickly sort out who I could learn from on the team. I did not pretend to know what to do—I put the offer out there that I needed help. I found people who helped the team and me think differently, who wanted to push, who had an entrepreneurial spirit. There was one person who was influential with the group, had insight into the issues faced, and had a passion to do whatever it took. Without teaming with him it would have been a long road. I learned so much from him, and with him thrust into an elevated role, he contributed so much to our growth. Along the way, I became an important mentor to him. A few years after I left, he was promoted to my position.

Use Tough Love: Push Others to Use Their Seat

But being included isn't always comfortable, and sometimes you have to push others to take their seat at the table. Susan Grimbilas recounted how she was once in a meeting, speaking quite fast, as she had a habit of doing, and therefore not making her point clearly. During the break, I asked her to chat outside the room.

"You have a seat in this room," I said. "Now use it well. You are nervous, you are speaking fast, you are not delivering your points, you are diminishing your own impact! Remember, you are included here because you belong here, you are an important contributor, and you can make a difference. Now go back in that room and act like it!"

She later admitted that had hurt. She was upset, frustrated, and quite frankly mad, but my feedback had been right on:

> It was delivered by you, I knew, with deep care for me and my contributions. It was clear to me that you wanted me to know that I was purposefully included. I had worked hard to earn a seat at that table.
>
> It moved me, Joe. It wasn't just that you told me to take the seat I had been given; it was that you didn't have to give me feedback, but you did. You put yourself out there for me, and that was powerful. As you know, that set you and me on a course for a trusted relationship that worked for both of us to this day.

Some may think it was a high-risk move in our relationship for me to provide such blunt, direct, tough-love feedback—to call out so clearly how Susan was diminishing herself. I understood the risk I took to share this feedback, and I did it knowingly and without benefit to myself. I deeply respected Susan's contributions to our leadership team and championed her career development, and I wanted her to be a full participant at that table. I could have let it go, I could have told her nicely, I could have told her in code and hoped she would sort it out . . . but those tactics are not my style. And I don't think they would have yielded the desired result for Susan.

If you are going to give someone a seat at a table, you may have to help them leverage it to their own advantage. Whether it's by kindly calling on them, even if they are uncomfortable, or giving them a kick in the rear to be all they can be, it is partly on you to maximize their contributions. As for Susan: she did take that seat at the table and went on to be a great COO and head of HR in North America and, later, head of HR globally.

CALL TO ACTION

Arthur Sprogis, recruiting marketing manager at BCG, shared how at times, he and his colleagues aren't even sure why they're in the room, but the invitation makes them feel good. They get to see the larger picture and feel respected and included. Their "minds become unlocked" as they begin to think beyond their roles and space, which opens up new possibilities in terms of how they might contribute, who else they might team up with, and where else they can go beyond their present roles. But Arthur also noted it is up to the leader to create the environment to make all that work. The following are some suggested actions.

Build a Regular Practice; Broaden Your Tables

Time is always a challenge, but if you build an inclusive mindset into your day-to-day and take a little prep and thinking time in advance of key meetings, the time obstacles simply melt away into your regular planning and preparation processes.

CALL TO ACTION

Sit back for a few minutes at the start of each week or month to think about the meetings you will be leading. What are the topics? Who will be attending? Ask yourself whom you can include who has additive expertise or a relevant but likely different point of view from yours, or who sees the organization from an entirely different viewpoint. Invite them!

Create an Environment Where All Are Included

Some may feel quite uncertain about being in the room and wonder why they are even there. This was described to me by my executive assistant and very close friend, Mary Kate Steincke:

During my early days at BCG, each time I was co-located with you, I tried to understand the role you wanted/expected me to play in your day-to-day—sit at my desk and only speak when spoken to, follow you around all day without real purpose, or some sort of in-between?

I will never forget one experience. After a meeting it was time for your next call. We walked together toward the office where you were sitting, and you asked, "Are you joining this call with me?" It was a weekly regional-chair-and-finance-team call. I replied, "I wasn't planning to, but I can if you want." The response was "Of course, you should join." And, at the start of the call, I was introduced.

This seems like a silly interaction, but to me at twenty-two years old, I thought it was the most thrilling opportunity. I also understood that the invitation and opportunity was not just for me to sit there and mindlessly listen to others speak; this was a real "seat at the table," and I felt empowered to earn my seat.

These actions—being invited to take a seat with you and then being introduced—made me feel welcome, important, special, relevant—truly part of the team.

I have to admit, I did not consciously think I was doing anything special. It just seemed logical and practical to have Mary Kate in the room with me. The more she was included in what I did, the better she could support me. But there was also value to Mary Kate. Over the years, she has become one of BCG North America's most respected executive assistants and moved into an additional role while supporting me: leading our North America executive-assistant training (creating content, delivering trainings), which will lead to new and different opportunities for her continued growth and development, and contributions to BCG, after I retire.

CALL TO ACTION

Set a reminder in your calendar to get to the meeting early. When you're there—whether it's in person or in a video setting—greet the participants, in particular the newcomers and the least tenured. Ask them something about themselves and say something about yourself (but do not dominate) to open others up. You might even personally offer refreshments or otherwise make sure the participants feel they are part of the meeting and are comfortable before it even begins.

Get People Talking

Once the meeting has begun, your job is to draw everyone into the conversation. Encourage dialogue and discussion to tease out the best information. Alex Gorsky, executive chairman of Johnson & Johnson, said, "You do not have to be the smartest in the room, but you have to get the smartest answer out of the room."[4]

CALL TO ACTION

As the meeting progresses, take inventory of who is participating and who isn't. Reach out to those who aren't contributing, specifically inviting their input. Recognize that some may be very uncomfortable, and be thoughtful about their situation, but do not let their discomfort hold you back from spurring their engagement.

Let Them Run

Recognize value by giving your teams the time and space to contribute. Being included when the stakes are highest, being free to leverage and stretch our capabilities and insight, and being allowed to contribute unique experiences will motivate and inspire any of us.

When Joanne Crevoiserat took over as CEO of Tapestry in July 2020, in the middle of the first year of COVID-19, she had to reenergize and revitalize her brands, and her entire fashion house, in a very challenging market. One thing she knew she had to do at the outset was increase the participation of many of her team members and get more voices included in the thinking on how to drive Tapestry forward, especially in that uncertain and complex global environment. When I asked her to share with me some of her thoughts on empowering her teams on her journey, she told a story about one of her early roles at Kaufmann's department stores:

> The sooner a new leader learns they must empower others, the better. When you are young, you don't typically realize this. You are energetic. You want to get things done fast. You think you can stay up all night, figure it out, and get it done yourself. You do not think as much of including others in the solutions, especially those you may not normally turn to.
>
> When I was an assistant controller at Kaufmann's department store, I had several teams reporting to me: accounting, sales audit, expense planning, financial planning, and analysis. I also had a new son at home with whom I naturally wanted to devote my time. I had a compelling reason to be home, and not always at work.
>
> I recall very well this learning moment. We had a problem in sales audit with one of our gift-card corporate partners, and one of my team leaders was a go-getter, in it to win. He had a strong team, and he liked to work with them. One day he came to me with an elegant solution. In fact, he and his team had already built a system to solve the problem. I would never have thought to even ask him to solve it, presuming they were buried in the day-to-day (and I was still learning about empowering my teams). That was when a light bulb went off. It was my role to nurture (my son and

my team), set goals, include everyone in our quest, give time and space, and then let 'em run.

CALL TO ACTION

When planning your agenda, set aside time for the participants to bounce ideas around without your input. You may even leave the meeting for a few minutes to give them the freedom to explore without fear of judgment.

FINAL THOUGHTS

The generous leader empowers by including many. I have also grown and developed, as a leader and as a person, by actively including others. A great coach once told me she knew no one else who could, or would, bring such a collection of uniquely experienced people into a meeting like I did. I asked what she meant.

Well, as an example, you had a very atypical set of participants helping you to prepare for your first speech as head of BCG's North America region, which you were about to present to the North America–wide four-hundred-plus-person officer team at the upcoming worldwide officer meeting. Present were your chief of staff, me (your coach), your executive assistant, one trusted officer, your wife, and your meeting logistical planner. You have to admit that was not your typical senior level "trusted" inner circle to help you plan for a major business presentation! And then, think about what you heard at that meeting. Wisdom from your executive assistant about how some of the things you said might feel to others. Admonishment from your wife to tone it down in parts. An idea from yet another advisor to bring other voices into the room, during your speech, to share the limelight.

The practice of inclusion may not have come to me naturally at first, but I have learned over time that by inviting voices into the room—voices beyond my inner circle and even a few unexpected ones—I will be pushed to question myself *and* I will be better positioned to push the organization to its greatest success.

How do you know whether you are taking the steps to motivate through inclusion?

In their 2017 *Global Human Capital Trends* report, after asking 600 survey respondents to rate and review 105 leaders, Deloitte was clear on the steps a leader must take and the remarkable impact leaders can have on empowerment when doing so.[5] When leaders value diverse points of view, listen to learn, are humble about what they do not know, have an open mindset about others' experiences, and enable all to engage, they are rewarded with a 17 percent increase in perceived team performance, a 20 percent increase in decision-making quality, and a 29 percent increase in collaboration.

Once you have started to incorporate the tools described in this chapter, your team members will begin to feel more empowered and believe they can contribute beyond their own present area of expertise, beyond where they are slotted in the organization. I'm talking about an expansive possibility in their minds about their own potential.

Empowerment through inclusion can also be a significant talent multiplier for you and your organization. You will become more efficient and more confident at delegating. You'll be more effective in your meetings, and your team will generate more creative solutions. You also get the best information. By including those on the front line or those who did the financial analysis, you gain access to the unvarnished truth without any sugarcoating or embellishment. You get the honest, simple facts you need to use in your decision-making.

The magic of collaboration will become apparent: in a diverse working group, you never know where a solution or inspiration might come from. Your team will know you are there supporting them, that you have their backs, and you'll continue to look for opportunities for them to grow and excel.

5

STAND UP FOR THEM

The Generous Ally

In today's *Fortune* 500 companies, half of the managerial positions are held by women—a big step forward from 20 years ago, when 75 percent of managers were men and only 25 percent women. However, 71 percent of these managers are still white, and in the C-suite, 86 percent are white and male. Many groups of our citizens are underrepresented in corporate ranks; people of color make up only 6 percent of that group, and only 1 percent of CEOs are Black.

Leaders who want to lead from the heart must recognize the ongoing disparity between the makeup of our executive leadership and our population as a whole. Structural disadvantage—the result of society-wide and historical discrimination and inequities—continues to be a systemic problem limiting opportunities for much of our workforce. This should go without saying, but developing yourself as a generous and therefore effective leader means supporting the diversity goals of your organization and advocating for greater representation by people of all ethnic backgrounds, races, gender and sexual identities, abilities, and so on. As a caring and compassionate leader, you have an opportunity to have a profound impact on the success of diverse individuals within your organization. You can become an action ally.

I am aware that my point of view is from a position of power and privilege, and some might think my perspective of what an ally is might carry a tone of a "white hero." I definitely do not want to think of myself as that. And to help ensure that I've got a balanced perspective in writing this chapter, I solicited input and feedback from many colleagues.

The lessons I have heard:

- "Will you shut up and simply listen, please."
- "Please do not try to imply you understand."
- "This is not the time to solve it for me; just open up a chance for me."
- "It is not an equal opportunity for all; would you please work to understand that? It is not on me to train you."
- "Let me be more me in your world; I am always code-switching for you."
- "I appreciate you go beyond just talking about being there for people. You actively work to create opportunities for me to thrive based on my skills and abilities, even putting me in situations that stretch those capabilities."
- "Please don't let your fear of making a mistake or being vulnerable stop you from taking action."

Being an ally is something that people do in support of others, and as my colleagues have said, a true ally is one who stands by another's side, who listens without pretending they walk in another's shoes or, worse, thinking they know what it means to walk in another's shoes. True allies are there for another; they are present. An *action* ally goes one step further and acts as a "coconspirator," offering additional support through action, as appropriate, by creating opportunities and clearing paths, but not by doing the work. They respond when asked. They don't run the other way if it gets difficult. They are willing to take personal risks. And I believe this willingness to take personal risks, this selflessness on behalf of another, is one of the greatest acts of generosity.

SECOND-NATURE ALLY

Two colleagues were in a client meeting. Both were partners: one a woman, one a man, the man much more senior. As they were getting set to present their information, one of the participants addressed the woman.

"Will you be sure to take notes?"

(Sadly, this type of occurrence has been described to me, or I have observed it, too often—the immediate assumption that the woman in a room is the note-taker, not the content expert, nor even a leader.)

Her colleague immediately chimed in. "Nope, I will take the notes. Michelle is the expert on this topic; she will be leading the conversation."

Michelle found the moment in the room fascinating. Several clients did not even notice what had just happened. One was a bit (negatively) shocked, and another, she could tell, was quite impressed.

After the meeting, acknowledging the risk he had taken, she thanked her male colleague for what he had done in that room—recognizing her contribution, clearing the path for her. As she told me, he barely registered what he had done. Not because he was naive, but rather because he simply lives as an action ally. He sees himself as someone who clears paths for others.

Marin Gjaja, chief customer officer for Ford's Model e (electric-vehicle portfolio), was that male colleague, and he has supported many successful women on their career journeys:

> I decided many years ago that I wanted to ensure that all I mentored, and women in particular, had a fair and equal playing field. As time went on, I became intentional about it: creating bonds, actively working to create opportunities for them, becoming their allies. It was the "right thing to do." It grew them, and it led to better results for my teams. I grew to believe it was one of the places I could really make a difference in making the institutions in which I work a better place. Over time it became second nature.

Some leaders wear the button during the recognition month. Some aim to promote the careers of those less privileged if it means achieving metrics-driven targets. But these leaders are *performative* allies; they do what is expected for the optics, maybe even telling themselves it's enough.

From my point of view, and this is an important distinction to make here, true allyship is when you see the other's talents and clear a path for them to elevate themselves toward continued success. It's when you become an accomplice as they pursue opportunities. It's when you are focusing on the person, not the organization.

What is required of you to do this work? A commitment to self-awareness. A willingness to make mistakes. A desire to be better and do better. Most importantly, humility and deep compassion. When you act generously to stand up for others, you do the following:

- elevate all voices;
- clear a path for another person;

- do a selfless thing for another human being;
- broaden everyone's views.

Rather than tell you what it means from my perspective—because really the meta point here is that you have plenty of that, even though, yes, this is my book!—you will read in the coming pages the effects of allyship, and its impact, from people whose voices must be elevated.

THE CHALLENGE: LOOKING IN THE MIRROR

This is a big ask, taking on the challenge of this work. It's a layered, complex, and sensitive subject that is much easier to avoid than to face—and when I write that it's a challenge, I'm obviously implying the challenge for white people. For some, they are simply comfortable with the way it is. If you do want to dive in, you may be uncomfortable or unsure about what is expected, how to start, and, sadly, how to even begin a conversation on the challenges and how you can help. You may simply be afraid of saying the wrong thing, even if your intention is true. You may not know what it means to be action oriented as it relates to allyship. You may not have even heard the term.

I will admit, when someone pointed out to me that they thought I was an action ally, I didn't really know what that meant or fully recognize what actions I was taking. For many years, I was one who said I was "color blind" and insisted that everyone had a shot. It's a meritocracy, right? Sure, it's easy to be color blind when you are white and a member of the majority in most rooms. But I was completely naive to the structural disadvantages facing many.

A dear friend—Jim Lowry, a Black leader in the consulting industry—pushed me hard when I took on my first office-leadership role. He made very clear the challenges faced by many and the opportunity and obligation I had to make a difference. Even as I began to push myself, I was acting on instinct, rather than with intention, and only after reaching for greater self-awareness, and more deeply understanding and connecting with colleagues' challenges, did I begin to understand the opportunity and work needed to get there. A meaningful turning point for me was at dinner with a set of colleagues. The Black midlevel manager at the table said to me, "Joe, do you even get it? I walk out the door each day on the way to the office wondering if I will get shot along the way." While it has been a journey, it was only as I listened in and learned more of others' lived experiences that I was able to become consistently intentional about advocating for people.

You may also be thinking you're not in a role or position to help others, to give them opportunities. The question to ask yourself is this: Are you hiding behind this reality to avoid looking at or dealing with the challenge of advocating for others? There is so much you can do, at whatever level—listening, being there, creating and supporting opportunities—and you do not have to be the CEO to do that.

THE RESEARCH: EVERYONE BENEFITS

The benefits of effective allyship with people of diverse backgrounds are well documented:

- A BCG Canada study found that people of diverse backgrounds who have an ally at work are twice as likely (~60 percent versus ~30 percent) to feel their work environment is free of bias versus those who do not have an ally.[1]
- The same study found that those same individuals who have allies perceive obstacles to advancement less than one-third as often as those without allies.

The 2020 *State of Allyship Report* done by Empovia (formerly Change Catalyst) reported the power of allyship.[2] Not surprisingly, they found that 92 percent of people with allies find it valuable for their career. When people have at least one ally, they are twice as likely to be satisfied with their job as those with no ally, 1.8 times more likely to be satisfied with their workplace culture, and 1.8 times more likely to feel they belong at their workplace. Overall, employees feel happier and more engaged, and productivity is improved.

This book is about elevating your leadership style by being more generous in the way you lead. But it is also about performing. As a leader, you could be the nicest person in the world, but if you do not deliver the numbers, you will not have the opportunity to use that heart. Management Leaders of Tomorrow, BCG, and other consulting firms have taken deep looks at the benefits of diversity in the workforce, and the evidence is clear: diversity helps the bottom line. Studies showed the following:

- companies with above-average diversity in their leadership teams enjoy 9 percent higher EBIT (earnings before interest and taxes) performance;[3]
- companies ranked in the top quartile in racial and ethnic diversity deliver 35 percent higher financial returns;[4]
- companies with at least 30 percent of leadership roles filled by women report 6 percent higher net margins.[5]

I could cite study after study showing that supporting diversity helps the individual and the organization. But the key to making diversity work is creating an atmosphere of allyship.

HOW TO BECOME AN ACTION ALLY

How do you begin to do this essential work? There are a number of
action steps that you can take to begin your own journey.

First, Just Listen

Of course, you must take action, but to start you need to just listen.
Let's circle back to what we discussed earlier: you do not know what
you do not know. To support people who have life experiences that
are far different from your own, you need to recognize that. You do
not know their lives, their battles, or their aspirations. And they don't
want you to pretend you know. Even more, they want you to do the
work to learn and understand as fully as you can by making the effort yourself—by asking and listening.

Brian Gross, a dear friend and colleague who rose to become BCG
North America COO (head of HR and operations), started his
career as a consultant, and one of his many roles over the years was
to serve as business-services team lead of the LGBTQ+ network
Pride@BCG. I asked him to share some of his thoughts on what it
means to be a good ally.

> A good ally is one who shows up and shuts up. They listen, they are
> present.
>
> Some think allyship is spewing worldly advice. Not so! Good
> allies recognize real differences in life experience. They do not pre-
> tend to get where I'm coming from, and they do not try to ex-
> plain to me who I am. They just accept me.
>
> They also show genuine curiosity. For example, they might ask
> what it looks like when one celebrates Ramadan as a Muslim, or
> Kwanzaa or Juneteenth as an African American. They ask, they
> probe, they are interested.

They will stand with me and be there consistently. They allow me to be me.

Vulnerability as a human also enables being a good ally. Being able to recognize challenges and not trying to explain them away, or always having solutions, is important, especially if you don't walk in the other's shoes.

In addition to listening and trying to know who I am, a good action ally uses that understanding to help pave the best opportunities for me, and then, of course, shows that they care about my progress.

Let me be clear about what being an action ally *isn't*: It isn't about jumping to the solution. And it's not about supporting me just so you can hit some metrics.

Susan Grimbilas also said good allies get to know the people they are supporting and demonstrate interest in their lives. They put the individual first—over the organization, over themselves, over their own personal desires—and they encourage individuals to "ultimately follow their hearts."

See the Individual

It is easy to lump people who appear to be alike into one group: people of one skin color, people of one ethnic background, people of a particular gender identity or sexual orientation. But that is naive—and hurtful. Reducing someone to one aspect of their identity can be harmful. When you know and see people as unique individuals, with rich sets of intersectional experiences, you can partner with them to create new opportunities.

Arthur Sprogis emphasized how important it is to avoid painting people with one brush. "People are different," he said. "A Black person might be Nigerian, Haitian, or Black American, and they should not be treated as a single checked box on a form." Arthur's allies don't see him simply as a gay, Hispanic man, with no idea where he comes from. Moreover, he cautioned, leaders seeking to serve as allies should not view their role as the solution. It's not about them: "You are not the prime mover; I am. But open the door, create a possibility that was previously excluded, and let me walk through. If you set it up, then I can keep moving forward on my own."

Fran Katsoudas, from Cisco, described a moment when she realized how she needed to make changes: "I've always considered myself an ally, but I had an important 'aha' moment when I was speaking with some LGBTQ+ colleagues about what people may assume about the LGBTQ+ community. From that conversation, I realized I had not taken enough time to learn and understand terms, legislation, history—the complexities. I started to reeducate myself. I moved from a position of not knowing to bringing curiosity to the work. I realized to be an ally I can't just show up. I also have to do the work."

Give Them Your Best

Fran said that to be the best ally she could be, she had to do the work—and that's true for all of us. If you are going to be a good ally, you must be at your best. Give time, be intentional, be there at the toughest moments. You learn the person's needs, you create opportunities, and you elevate their talents. You are also expected to help guide the way through when asked.

In Patrick Grzanka, Jake Adler, and Jennifer Blazer's qualitative interviews with allies, respondents reported that allyship must be *active*, not passive, to be truly effective.[6] That means allies should be truly motivated to enact real change, instead of only generally supporting minority rights without taking specific actions to achieve this goal.

Justin Dean, BCG senior partner and head of BCG's Northeast System, has had firsthand experience with structural disadvantages:

I do not need *you* to tell me how hard it is to be Black. I do not need sympathy, so do not pretend to be me.

An ally is going to try to understand the shoes you walk in, knowing they have never worn those shoes, and they give you space for you to be you. They also stay with you. You see some people put on a good face and then retreat; after all, it's easy to support someone when it costs you nothing. But an ally is there when the rubber hits the road. They will put themselves in awkward positions to empathize with you. They will make personal sacrifices for you.

What I really need, from an ally, is the best you. . . . Ask yourself how you're investing your best quality time, your best training in the other person. I need your top 5 percent for the time you spend coaching me. And to give me your top 5 percent, you must also share some of your failures; you must express some vulnerability to build connection, to really help.

Justin's ask for one's best goes much deeper than a surface request, and I must admit it may not even be until writing this book that the gravity of what he was saying landed. What he said: share your failures, your vulnerabilities, your fears, because they show you are willing to give me something more—something real. I'm asking you to think of me as an equal. I'm asking you to level the playing field. I am asking you to stick with it, even in the most difficult moments. That is your top 5 percent, and it will build something meaningful.

CALL TO ACTION

Becoming an effective ally takes time and work, but we don't need to reinvent the wheel. Those who have walked this path, including many of my trusted colleagues, have discovered several tried-and-true steps to make it happen.

Take Advantage of Opportunities (If There Is Interest)

It's not always easy to figure out who needs or wants an ally, and even those who you think could benefit from an ally may not have the same perspective. Often it develops naturally through a working relationship that grows close. Sometimes you find yourself opening a door for another, not really sure if they want that door opened or not. You want to help, but you will have to find your own personal path into starting.

CALL TO ACTION

Look at the relationships you have developed or are developing. Observe relationships where you find yourself helping create opportunities for another. Are you serving as an ally in a relationship that started with intentional choice or one that has developed and evolved over time? If the relationship has evolved over time, consider stepping back and having a conversation about their interest in your support and how to make that support most valuable to them.

Practice Perspective Taking

As my colleagues suggested, you can't pretend to know those you are supporting or what they have gone through or are going through. Rather, you must listen to learn and work to understand their aspirations.

This suggestion is to do less talking and more listening. But you may ask, how do I open a conversation? First off, of course, you have to be attentive and respectful, but not intrusive (I realize this sounds tricky). Try inviting and open-ended, conversation-starting questions like, "How are you doing?" "What is working well for you at XYZ company?" Be willing to share something real about yourself, and please be willing to admit you do not know it all.

CALL TO ACTION

For those you find yourself supporting, either explicitly or not, talk about what your allyship might look like. Prepare for the meeting. Ask thoughtful questions about their experiences and, importantly, just listen. Learn about their perspectives, their aspirations. Be ready to share some of your own vulnerabilities to open the relationship.

Continually Reassess

As with any role, your level of success and effectiveness is not something to be assumed or taken for granted. With the help of the person you are supporting, you need to periodically assess the work you are doing and ensure you are making a difference.

Ian Pancham led BCG's Black and Latinx network for five years. From his perspective, an ally "helps to give you access—a seat at the table, and then pushes you to use your voice, to test, to take chances, to develop and grow. They do not do it; they help set it up, and then they trust." The other big thing, he said, is time: "Those who care give attentive time. They show up, they hear me, and *then* they coach. I have had some mentors who think they are mentors, but I always get canned answers to my situation. They did not listen; they made no effort to understand."

Ian recounted a story to me: "Joe, you were one of the first to actually push me to use my voice. I had a seat at a key BCG table, but I was 'sitting back.' You told me, 'Ian, you are there because we trust you—speak up, push us, drive us to take action.' This was powerful;

you were not berating me, and it came from a place of caring, but you were pretty clear!"

CALL TO ACTION

Set up periodic check-ins with your ally and ask for feedback:

- Am I opening paths toward opportunities?
- Am I supporting you along the path you've chosen without doing the work for you or telling you what to do?
- Am I helping you achieve your goals?
- Am I with you in your tough times?
- Is our mutual work creating positive impact for you? For the organization?
- Am I taking the action needed to encourage you to move forward if you are hesitant?

Check Yourself: Are You Retreating When the Times Get Tough?

This question of whether you are there during tough times, rather than ducking out, is so important that it deserves a callout. What does this mean? Say the person you are supporting underdelivers on a project or doesn't get promoted as they had hoped. Or maybe they are in line to get promoted, but the team's leaders have some questions about the prospect. I can go on and on, and you can also imagine other tough circumstances. This is the key time when you need to fully have your ally's back.

Kedra Newsom, cohead of BCG's Center for Inclusion and Equity, noted that allies must be willing to take risks and to use their positions and power to drive action. They need to offer support by "shaping, providing tough feedback, guiding, making space . . . truly being a coconspirator."

CALL TO ACTION

Do a periodic self-reflection. Has the person you are supporting faced some tough times recently? Were you there for them personally? Were you on their side, publicly or behind the scenes, to help keep opportunities open? Did you duck the challenge? Did you presume it would just work out?

Give Your Top 5 Percent

You are supporting someone with great talent that is not always recognized, and your actions must be real. Everything you do must come from the heart, and you also must be *all in*.

CALL TO ACTION

Be sure that you give your best.

- Set up regular meetings and honor them, resisting the temptation to reschedule when conflicts arise.
- Show up on time, having prepared with the same degree of effort you would for other meetings.
- Listen to whatever they have on their agenda for the session.
- Share a personal story relating to their concern, one that illustrates your authenticity and vulnerability.
- Learn their longer-term aspirations.
- Be on the constant lookout for opportunities you can open for the person.
- Discuss how you can support ensuring that path is available.
- Take action to ensure the path to the opportunities is open and available.
- Do not just talk about it but make the moves to help make it real. Go out on a limb if you must.

Broaden Your Efforts

Clinical psychologists and researchers Glenda Russell and Janis Bohan discuss institutional allyship for LGBTQ+ equality in their work published in the *Journal of Social Issues*.[7] They define first-order change as relatively superficial, stating that it aims to modify existing practices without challenging "institutional structures or hierarchies of power and privilege." On the other hand, second-order change is "foundational change; it works to alter structures and challenge hierarchies of power."

While I have been talking about supporting individuals within the organization, which—although valuable—may be considered first-order change, we can scale our allyship efforts and have far-reaching impact well beyond the individual. According to Ian Pancham, "The best mentors do not just support the person; they use their organization to help move the world" by using their access, position, and power.

For me, this scaling began as I was running an office. My mentor, Jim Lowry, introduced to me the differences I should try to make within my office with, for example, recruiting, retention, and inclusion. While I was running the West Coast System, two colleagues, Danny Acosta and Brian Gross, meaningfully raised my awareness of code-switching and the fear that many have of open, productive conversations. This led to an idea while I was North America chair to run a Deliberate Discourse Dinners series where tables of six to eight diverse BCGers engaged in a facilitated conversation on race. As my scope expanded, Justin Dean, a dear friend with whom the coaching has been mutual, opened my eyes to broader opportunities for the organization and the need for an ecosystem of partners to make a real difference in the racial-equity space. This led me to join CEO Action for Diversity and Inclusion and BCG's team helping to drive the Southern Communities Initiative in 2022.

The Southern Communities Initiative is an organization founded by Vista Equity Partners, PayPal, and BCG that works to make a difference in six Southern communities where about half of the entire US Black population resides and where economic inequalities are sizable. One of its initiatives is to address the digital divide. During a visit to Charlotte, we saw an excellent example of the importance of an ecosystem. The effort started with a huge donation of laptops to the community by a national corporation, but those computers were only step one—and by themselves they were woefully insufficient. People needed to benefit from them, and a consortium of organizations in Charlotte worked together to advertise the availability of the laptops, distribute them, educate users on how to use them, provide computer support, and offer job-training and placement services so those who received the computers could use them to better their situation. In other words, the initiative required people, organization, and time, which an ecosystem of players in Charlotte pulled together.

A first-level corporate ally might donate computers; this would reflect passive allyship. But the "full action ally" corporation would seek to understand the communities and their needs and either fund the entire value chain (rare, and not expected, given the project doesn't necessarily fit with the corporation's typical expertise) or team with others to ensure everything gets done. The full action ally is willing to invest patient capital and help fund, or provide, capacity and capability building. This action ally is willing to invest not because they expect any direct financial profit or payback but because they know the ultimate return will be the economic development of the communities and all the positive things that will result.

CALL TO ACTION

Influence your organization and beyond.

- Identify specific opportunities to drive diversity, equity, and inclusion objectives within your leadership purview, and then select and put a process in place to move forward on one to two opportunities.
- Offer your support to initiatives in your broader organization that are of interest to you.
- Volunteer your time to a cross-industry diversity, equity, and inclusion effort of interest to you.

FINAL THOUGHTS

Allyship is a personal and professional mandate because there aren't that many different people in the room. The reality is, it's likely that most rooms you are in are at least 50 percent white, especially—as noted in the introduction to this chapter—as you climb higher in any large organization. That's why you might think you are color blind, or why it never occurs to you that someone might get shot on their way to work. How would you know if you have never even talked to someone of color, especially about something real? Because there are almost always fewer people of color in any executive room you are in, it's harder to get those perspectives, and the mission of inclusion is to change that. And the effects are a series of cascading and infinite benefits that begin with your humility and the thoughtful and selfless actions you take to elevate another person. You can be an ally at any level of leadership. You can be an ally at any moment of any day, anywhere. The data are also clear. Studies repeatedly show that when organizations leverage the most diverse teams, the financial results are superior. Studies also make it clear that when someone facing structural disadvantages has a true ally, they enjoy greater job satisfaction, feel more engaged, are happier at work, and report being more productive.

Growth is uncomfortable. We often learn more from our mistakes than we do from our successes. But the stakes are high when you are talking about someone's life. In moments, and with opportunities, as important as these, I believe you should stretch. Rather than retreating or defaulting to defensiveness, or inaction, as you are supporting another and the going gets tough, take the chance, be uncomfortable, let yourself grow. There is a vulnerability to allyship, and this is in the true spirit of being a generous person and a great leader.

It's awkward to simplify what I believe to be an imperative as a human being to act on behalf of others. It is even more uncomfortable to go beyond and explain that while doing these things should be, and is, enough, there are also exponential benefits to you and your organization. Together you will uncover better solutions to tough challenges, driving better business outcomes. The face of management is slowly changing, and, by advocating for others, you have an opportunity to be part of this widespread change.

But, of course, there are many others you support in your role. Let's explore how you can move forward to recognize *all* of them, celebrating what they have accomplished, looking forward to further contribution, and overall unlocking and inspiring everyone's potential.

6

RECOGNITION AND FEEDBACK

Generous Development

People want to be recognized for what they are doing. They want to get better at it, too. A key role of the leader, then, is to first recognize potential and then help people fully develop that potential by showing consideration and respect for them—and for their work contributions—and by creating opportunities for them to further grow. This includes both the individuals who work directly for you and others beyond your direct reports.

Each of us wants to be seen.

What does that mean? The gift of recognition is taking a real interest in someone's work, paying attention to detail, setting your own ego aside, and celebrating another's effort and achievement. You must really see what they achieved and genuinely want them to build on what they do best. I bristle at the idea of celebrating "effort" just for the sake of doing. It sounds like a participation trophy, and I believe in driving toward results. But the two are not mutually exclusive. When you applaud someone's effort sincerely, you are validating their hard work, and that makes people feel seen.

What it also does is make it possible to unapologetically drive toward solutions *without* a participation trophy. I am a huge believer, as are nearly all the leaders I interviewed, that the best feedback is delivered promptly, clearly, directly, and honestly, even bluntly. It is candidly telling it like it is, addressing critical and potentially very tough topics, but also calling out and helping people to leverage their strengths. You give this feedback in service to the betterment of the person receiving it—to advance their opportunities.

When you recognize and deliver constructive feedback from the heart, truly caring about those you are coaching, the benefits are plentiful:

- people feel seen and respected;
- people take pride in what they do and are inspired to go beyond what they thought they could.

Think about a hard thing you did and how you stood a little taller after accomplishing it—the pride and confidence it built. As a leader it's important that you generously help people tap into their pride and confidence; validate the ways they are exceptional, push them to take on new challenges, and tell them clearly how they can be better. When you do all of these things in a large-hearted and benevolent way, you are both personally and professionally developing someone. You are helping them to take a much more expansive vision of their own opportunities and growth. For you as a leader, that has obvious compounding effects, as the more potential people see in themselves, the more ambitious and hardworking they become.

WORDS THAT INSPIRE FOR A LIFETIME

Susan Grimbilas recounted to me a powerful story about recognition from her earlier working days. At age 29, when her company went through a massive reorganization, she described how she was promoted to a role she felt she had no business getting:

> I suddenly had four hundred people reporting to me. I was in waaaay over my head. One day I was meeting with my manager when he looked at me and said, "You are simply the best I've ever seen." There wasn't a lot of fuss. It was just the two of us, so no public recognition. It doesn't meet the classic criteria for good feedback. It wasn't specific or action-oriented or any of that stuff. But twenty-five years later, I still remember how amazing it made me feel. On bad workdays, I still think about that episode, and it gives me strength and confidence. I would have moved mountains for that manager. He's long retired now, but to this day, I would do anything for him. Eight words is all it took.

This validation of her efforts, and the confidence the push inspired in Susan, propelled her into a fruitful and prolific career. This was in part due to the fact that she was asked to do something that she thought was a reach—she was asked to do a hard thing, and then when she did it successfully, she was recognized for it. That praise and recognition was powerful and motivating well beyond the role she was in at the time and inspired her to think more expansively about her role in that organization and her career going forward.

THE CHALLENGE: FINDING TIME AND COURAGE

The biggest challenges in recognition and development are investing the time it takes to build rapport and understand another's strengths and opportunities, and having the sensitivity, the self-awareness, and, importantly, the courage to deliver the message.

The first question to ask yourself is what you are trying to achieve. Are you trying to nurture your staff member's growth and enjoy the team's resultant performance? Or are you aiming for higher team performance and therefore your own reward?

When you commit to the individual's growth, you commit to time, which, for many of us, is too short. Time to get to know a person. Time to share recognition for a job well done. Time to reflect on their strengths and wrap those strengths into ideas for improvement. Time to think through how you will clearly and plainly deliver feedback and then to give it, sometimes in the moment.

THE RESEARCH: HONESTY AND CARE

As I noted in the introduction, BCG and the BVA Group surveyed 9,000 employees from around the globe in 2020 and 2021 about 18 qualities across head, heart, and hand characteristics. The survey found that two of the top four qualities people look for in their leaders are recognition (number one) and coaching and development (number two).

O.C. Tanner, a Great Place to Work–Certified advisory and people-development software company, conducted an employee-engagement study to evaluate the impact of a recognition culture on employee experience.[1] Their results, mirroring BCG's, pointed out the value of recognition. They analyzed 1.7 million employee survey responses gathered between 2018 and 2020 across small, midsize, and large companies, and the benefits were clear. People who feel recognized at work are 2.2 times more likely to say innovative thinking is embraced in their organizations and twice as likely to say people in their organizations are willing to go above and beyond.

The Leadership Circle Profile reports an 85 percent correlation to effectiveness for leaders who demonstrate *relating* skills, such as compassion and caring.[2] And according to executive coach Dana Theus, tough love, an important form of feedback, isn't about being mean; it's about being compassionate and clear, even when the feedback is neither fun nor easy to deliver.[3] Effective feedback, tough love or not, needs to come from a place of honesty and care.

And while the idea of managing people with greater care may still strike some leaders as being intrinsically weak, the Conference Board's ongoing employee-engagement research has proved that workplace leadership cannot succeed without it.[4] As the Conference Board report puts it, "What matters most to people is how they are made to feel by the bosses who manage them. So, demonstrate to your employees that they're authentically valued. Provide them with opportunities to grow and to contribute at a higher level. Appreciate their work. Make people feel they matter. Do all these things and more knowing it's rarely an appeal to our minds that inspires any of our greatest achievements."

As Scott Kirby said, feedback that is appropriately delivered can "build further trust, and even build pride in wanting to do better."

HOW TO MAKE ROOM FOR OTHERS TO THRIVE

As you develop your leadership skills, you are likely building your capacity both to recognize the people on your team and to give them feedback. But to do either of these effectively, you need to build relationships and a community within your team. You need to build rapport.

Rapport is built when recognition becomes an ongoing practice of positive reinforcement of strengths and acknowledgment of achievement and effort. That's what makes people truly feel seen and open to hearing what you have to say.

Then, when constructive feedback is delivered, it's seen by the recipient as a well-intended suggestion to enhance performance and not an exercise meant to criticize or deflate. It focuses on how the individual can leverage their strengths and how opportunities can be created for further growth.

Much has been made of the feedback sandwich, where you start with praise or recognition before delivering bad news, and then you close with something nice again. Although that technique is used when delivering specific criticism, the same theory can be applied in the bigger picture: you build the relationship around the positive, and then when the negative message has to be delivered, it's in the context of a good working relationship overall.

I had a fellow working for me who was excellent on so many dimensions: sensitive, understanding, clear, yet soft-spoken with a very high emotional intelligence. He was also focused and well organized, and he got things done. He had very high potential, and I wanted to see him climb in the organization. I believe he knew of his strengths, but he did not always display them with the confidence he deserved of himself. I am not sure he knew we saw them and valued them.

As I was considering him for a more senior line role, others asked me an important question: "OK, Joe, he is great on so many dimensions, but will he make the tough calls?" They typically only saw the calm, soft-spoken public side of him, so it was a fair question. It was critical that he understood we recognized all his strengths and that he knew they were his ticket to continued success. But I also had to ensure he understood that others were worried about him making the tough calls when warranted, and he would have to be aware of that. There was an added complexity to this particular situation that underscores my point about honest and sincere communication, and also developing rapport. This man was also an "out" gay man, so validating him and recognizing his strengths required additional sensitivity to ensure the feedback was received free of perceived identity judgments. His strengths were very real, but would he think I was only stereotyping? Would he worry if his strengths were even valued? Would he wonder if we valued his strengths on their merit? Would he shut down during feedback? I had to think it through carefully, plan thoughtfully, and have specific examples of how we recognized and valued his strengths. I was specific about the ways his skills propelled the organization, expedited decision-making, and helped me. Today he is in a leadership role in the company.

Give Clear, Honest, and Direct Feedback

You may worry about giving clear feedback that will cause pain. Or that might lead to people not liking you. But that is not the point; feedback is not about *you*. It's about helping another improve.

When what you convey is clear, honest, and direct—all the while wrapped in true care for the other individual's development—the potential pain will be at best a sting, not a bite. You can push people hard to grow to be their best when it is clear you care about them, showing respect for their growth and their development. When you are authentic, honest, and clear, treating people with respect, they will trust you.

In times of skepticism, disruption, and personal challenges, at those moments when the chips are down, if someone is straight—if one knows a leader is truly trying to help—trust is built.

I had a difficult feedback experience where, as hard as it was, I remained committed to clarity of message. A senior BCG leader, having done extremely well in his overseas home market, had transferred to the United States for an international experience. After a couple of years in the United States, he was struggling. He reported to me in my role as head of that particular office system, and although he had been working extremely hard to be successful in the US market, he struggled to create relationships with US clients. His European experience did not resonate with US companies, and he struggled a bit with the nuances of English (while his spoken English was fine). The day came when I called him into my office, sat him down, and delivered clear feedback: "You have three options: go home, quit, or I ask you to leave BCG." It was direct; it was blunt; it was said in those exact words.

How did that work out? It went over well. I had taken the time to get to know my colleague, and I could sense he was thinking the same thoughts—he was not happy underperforming. My message was delivered with nothing but care for him, and ultimately it was freeing for him. He went home and became a star again.

Avoid mushed feedback. Too many people, when they think someone needs feedback, mush up positives with the improvement areas, which risks leaving those receiving the feedback feeling OK across the board instead of feeling good about their strengths and clear on the areas needing improvement. I had a colleague who was great at team management and client engagement but poor with grammar and typos. While he got frustrated hearing it, it was very clear that he had to address the weakness, or it would hold him back in a business where written communication is key. It would have been useless if he had heard, "You are doing OK—just need to work on this one issue," versus, "You are exceptional with the teams and the client, but if you do not address the grammar and typos, your career will stall." Leaving people unclear about where they stand or what improvements need to be made serves no purpose. Steve Gunby noted that this "is not caring. It may feel safe, but . . . it is not helpful."

This practice takes, well, practice. Sometimes it requires courage to withstand the backlash for being too candid or blunt and to face the fear of being disliked or the accusation of stereotyping someone's strengths and thus appearing to diminish the person to a role. But perhaps more importantly, committing to other people's development takes a lot of thinking, effort, and confidence.

Focus on Strengths

Many CEOs speak of the importance of tapping into the strengths of their people to enable their organization to achieve its goals. Leveraging strengths for professional growth is no different from, and can actually be far more effective than, only focusing on people's shortcomings. Of course, leveraging strengths begins with identifying those strengths.

A manager once compared me to a colleague whom I'll call Frank: "Joe, if I put you or Frank in an empty room and asked you to solve an extremely tough problem on your own, Frank would come up with the answer, and you would struggle. But if I asked each of you to find the best people to team up with to execute the solution for that tough problem and actually get something done, Frank would be stuck, and you would get it done every time."

He used the tough-love approach, and it wasn't the most fun feedback I ever received. But he was also clear about the strengths he believed I could leverage—insight into others' strengths, the ability to build a highly functioning team, the ability to inspire others to contribute as team members while performing at their individual best, organization, and focus on outcomes. This inspired me to further tap into and grow my own strengths as I tackled new challenges going forward.

Studies by BRANDspeak, a leadership and talent-development firm, noted that feedback too often focuses on areas for development and does not recognize one's successes and strengths as much as it should.[5] As Lori Lepler, CEO of BRANDspeak, noted to me, "Too often we overlook the power of 'Strength-Based Development': The practice of deeply knowing an individuals' skills and capabilities and linking those strengths to priority AFD(s) [areas for development]to accelerate learning, growth, and performance." In fact, nearly two-thirds of employees report that their strengths are inadequately recognized and leveraged. And yet, when feedback acknowledges strengths and leverages them in overcoming weaknesses or developing new capabilities, an individual's growth is accelerated.

One BCGer said that working for a manager who had been trained in a strength-based development approach was very influential, as it helped them better understand how to improve and move forward: "Understanding my core strengths is much more helpful and encouraging than conversations that focus solely on areas for development in my current role."

No one wants to be beaten up or only criticized for all they've done wrong or should have done better. While it is obviously critical to lay out the areas where improvement is needed, identifying strengths—and coaching people on how to leverage those strengths to improve—produces far more effective feedback. And when all this is wrapped together with true care and interest, magic can be made.

CALL TO ACTION

Implementing a practice of regular recognition, strength identification, and effective feedback requires some forethought. Let me suggest some actions to help you get started.

Nurture Your Team

Think about the areas where you perform best. As you amass your own list, reflect on how you leveraged your strengths to grow in areas from a time when you weren't as strong or experienced. Why not do the same for those you are working with on developing themselves?

Take some time to think about those you are helping to improve and what you respect about them. Analyze their strengths, which can incorporate interpersonal relations, analytical capabilities, strategic thinking, and so much more. Then, as you formulate the feedback you want to deliver using that care and compassion—whether on the job or in annual performance reviews—you'll have the foundation of their strengths at the ready to help you assess potential development opportunities.

CALL TO ACTION

Spend some time thinking through *each* person on your team (plus those whom you may be mentoring outside your team or those who may be heading toward joining your team). Ask yourself if you're *really* engaging with them as much as you could be.

- When was the last time you told them what you appreciated about them?
- Have you had recent conversations with each of them about their aspirations?
- Where are they trying to improve?
- Where do you think they need to most improve?
- What, specifically, are you doing to actively work to recognize their strengths and weaknesses, and help them develop?

Go Deeper in Your Thinking

It's normal to get caught up in tactical evaluations of how an individual is performing, but true development involves weaving complex attributes together. It goes beyond the numbers.

CALL TO ACTION

Reflect further on each of the identified individuals.

- What are the metrics against which each person is currently being measured?
- What are the skill sets and capabilities that each individual can offer? How do those compare with the skills they're using for their current role?
- What is each person's set of strengths? How do they match up with their roles?
- What is each person's set of shortcomings? How do they prevent the person from achieving more success?
- Which strengths should you most encourage each person to use to improve on the shortcomings?
- What is the best way to convey your message when it's time to provide coaching and feedback?

Keep It Honest; Tough Love Is OK

You care deeply for your employees' development. You want them to grow. You want people to take advantage of their strengths. You also need to be clear on where they need to develop. As I noted, no one wants to hear mush. If they are going to be given suggestions on how to improve their performance, they need to understand clearly and viscerally their development needs.

Christina Sistrunk wasn't far into her career when it hit home for her: at the end of the day, it is all about people and talent, and you have an important role in helping them grow.

Some leaders think being tough on people will motivate them. Of course, that is not true, but it is also not all about rose petals and rainbows.

In my early thirties, I had a mentor who asked me, "Are you being driven by your concern for yourself or them?" Some leaders, operating from a place of fear—their own—focus on wanting to be liked. For those leaders it is scary, almost impossible, to have a heart-to-heart with someone about their development opportunities.

I learned over the years it is uncomfortable to give the tough, direct feedback, but you rehearse, you practice, you take chances and it becomes a lot easier . . . and, of course, when you see the benefit of watching others grow it becomes a whole lot easier.

CALL TO ACTION

As you prepare feedback, think through the words. Do you have vivid examples of both the good and the bad? Then practice your delivery, stepping back and listening to yourself. Are you abundantly clear in what you are saying? If you were in the employee's shoes, would you understand the improvement opportunities presented and the actions you'd need to take? If not, rethink the content and practice again.

Jump at Development Opportunities

The best feedback is generally in the moment, provided that all necessary information is readily available and those present are level-headed. When delivered in real time, feedback can often be far more explicit about the situation, with detailed explanations about what was observed. The recipient can relate to what is being said because the experience is still very fresh.

When I was a new 24-year-old Procter & Gamble sales manager, I had four sales reps reporting to me, and I rode the route with each rep every two weeks. I was doing the year-end review for one of them, a 42-year-old, having prepared all the points I thought he needed to hear—points of both opportunity and criticism. Somewhere along the way, he stopped me.

"Whoa, Joe, you ride with me every other week and I have never heard any of this. What is all that about?!"

It was simple: I had been too nervous to provide feedback in the moment, especially because I lacked confidence. When that painful session was over, my boss privately told me to never again provide annual feedback without the person already knowing each point I was going to make!

CALL TO ACTION

Commit to providing some level of immediate feedback every day, always keeping in mind the need to be clear, direct, and caring. And when it's time to give an annual performance review, be sure that nothing there will surprise the employee.

Build on Your Progress

Steve Gunby understood the importance of real-time feedback as well as the need to keep building on what he learned. One of his strategies was to come out of nearly every client meeting asking for a debrief. First, he would ask the team for feedback about how he did. True, people rarely stepped up with critical feedback on Steve's performance, but he showed he was working as a team, and he was part of it. Then he conducted a self-evaluation of his own performance, which was candid and often critical. Next, he would turn the spotlight onto the team members, asking how they felt *they* did individually and collectively. And, of course, he would provide feedback. It was not always fun, but the consistent two-way feedback, clear and in the moment, enabled his team members to constantly learn, develop, and grow.

CALL TO ACTION

Keep at this—keep looking for those moments where you can nurture your people through recognition and where you can provide honest feedback. Deliver your messages clearly, directly, and constructively, and regularly ask how it is going for them. Together, come to an agreement about how they will grow even further and how you can support them. And be sure you never surprise anyone in your formal feedback sessions!

And to keep it up, let me suggest a few actions:

- Depending on the feedback mechanisms in your organization, keep a simple running list of your people's strengths. It does not have to be elaborate; notes in your iPhone will work. Review them quarterly. Add to them. Use them in all reviews.
- While it may feel radical, once per quarter, over lunch or a cup of coffee, ask your employees for feedback on your development efforts with them. Do you engage real-time? Do you listen to their concerns? As you provide them with actions for improving, do you suggest their relevant strengths to leverage?
- Identify an activity in your business that you do with your team—selling meetings, client presentations, meetings with more senior executives—and make it a habit to have a real-time feedback session after such events.

FINAL THOUGHTS

Recognizing an individual is cited over and over as one of the top behaviors people look for in a leader. Seeing them, hearing them, knowing when they are excelling and why—and when they are falling short and why—is one of the most important things you can do for your employees. It shows you care; it is essential to making them even better. When you relay development opportunities to them, honestly and directly, with ways for them to grow and make a difference, you also build trust, respect, followership, and pride.

While recognition and development are powerful and fundamental practices, you can also make a difference with small gestures— small gestures that are really big gestures! They signal that you do mean it when you pay close attention to people and take action to show they matter. These actions create a lasting bond, even coming from the smallest old-school symbolic gesture, and they convey a thoughtfulness and generosity of spirit that people remember and appreciate.

7

SMALL ACTS, BIG IMPACT

Generous Moments

Remember the importance of the gold star at the top of your elementary school papers or drawings? Simple gestures can go a long way, even in the corporate world.

What do these simple gestures give another person? What do they say about us?

WHY IT MATTERS

Scott Kirby is a huge believer in the importance of small gestures. As he put it to me, "Small gestures matter infinitely more than the big gestures." A compelling example for him occurred during the pandemic. His wife was on a flight to Chicago, and the flight captain, a Black woman, was effusive about how much she loved United. Her enthusiastic loyalty stemmed from the George Floyd time period, when Scott had called multiple employees, including that particular captain, to check in on how they were doing. Remembering that call, she told his wife she would "do anything for United," because the

CEO had personally connected with her when it had mattered most.

Small gestures aggregate to represent something big. They show effort, thoughtfulness, and intention; they say I'm paying attention to you. YOU are important. In Scott's example, the action of the call was small and simple enough, but the subject matter of the call was raw and emotional and influential for the recipient, and thus created an indelible connection with Scott because he recognized this important moment and need, and he acknowledged it.

I believe that is true in the case of all small gestures, in one way or another. The key is this: it is a symbol or a gesture or a moment that marks an occasion meaningful to the recipient. The incongruity is what makes it exceptional: the birth of a child, a wedding, the death of a loved one—these are all pivotal moments in one's life, and their acknowledgment feels like a grand gesture but in fact requires very little effort on the part of the giver. What is the impact of these acts?

- They acknowledge someone at a critical moment in time *for them*—and that acknowledgment makes them feel important and understood.
- This acknowledgment makes them feel included, a critical part of the team, and part of a community.

The generous leader cultivates these practices because they show a level of attention to another person, because they show that that person matters. You are reading this book because you know that you must build these skills—not only because acts of generosity are selfless by definition but also because they will ultimately shape you into the leader your organization needs you to become.

As I have said many times already, you do not think of the secondary benefits when you take action to recognize pivotal moments in another's life. However, like all the selfless acts in this book, they have the effect of the virtuous cycle of goodness and will likely earn your employees' appreciation and bring you both joy. This appreciation creates a bond of loyalty, heightens employee retention, and boosts morale and pride in the organization.

THE CHALLENGE: COMMITTING AND BELIEVING

You may see many hurdles to making this practice work, and you will likely be tempted to suspend such small gestures now and then as hurdles surface.

- How do I make the time needed given how much I already have to scramble to get everything done?
- Do I really need to do this now that my team size has grown from 5 to 25 (to hundreds)?
- How do I *remember* to make these small gestures when I have so many other (seemingly) important things to do?
- For whom do I show these kindnesses—and where do I draw the line?
- Will it really make a lasting difference?

And I will say, this practice *can* be challenging.

As an example, I send a handwritten, personalized holiday card to everyone on my team each year—a small gesture to each individual. But it is a challenge. You may question the ambition of writing a short note, or whether it is even appreciated these days. But the challenge goes much further: I need the cards, addresses and stamps on the cards, prompt mailing, et cetera. A manageable task if leading a team of five or so, but as my teams have been growing, the challenge has grown. I will say, however, that the positive feedback and the added value to my relationships from making a very personal connection, which required visible effort, has been wonderful. Whether it be a paper holiday card that is considered special at this moment in time or a new form of a personal note in the future (that is visibly not AI generated), this personal touch will always be valued, so I will keep it up.

Leaders sometimes also worry about how small gestures will be received or perceived. Will their motives be questioned? Will the small gestures be viewed as too personal in today's sensitive work environment?

THE RESEARCH: PERSONAL AND PROFESSIONAL

Research about simple acts of kindness and other small gestures has shown multiple positive impacts. Happiness is boosted. Stress is reduced. Overall life satisfaction is improved, and a heightened general sense of well-being is fostered. Relationship bonds are strengthened.

HR consulting and people-software firm TINYpulse by Limeaid reported that simple gestures of kindness offer multiple benefits, including boosted morale, which in turn leads to increased productivity and efficiency in the workplace.[1] Moreover, a workforce that genuinely enjoys the work environment can help you attract top talent and keep retention high. Employees will feel more loyal to the company when they have a good and healthy work environment and when they feel more valued and supported.

As noted in a February 2020 *Psychology Today* article, "Classic research in organizational behavior conducted in the 1940s found that . . . small acts of kindness, appreciation, and recognition go a long way toward creating a climate of high performance."[2] This is not to suggest that normal motivating activities—for example, rewarding people for good performance—is unimportant. It simply highlights the fact that the casual, seemingly insignificant ways we treat and recognize people can sometimes play a bigger role in producing positive work attitudes and performance than the seemingly more businesslike, task-oriented activities many managers focus on, sometimes exclusively.

Researcher Adam Grant ran an experiment on what happened to the productivity of university fundraisers when a senior manager engaged in the small gesture of showing gratitude for their work.[3] The researcher had the director of annual giving visit the university and perform a seemingly minor deed—he personally thanked the telephone fundraisers for their efforts. Although perhaps a nice gesture, most people wouldn't consider this an example of particularly great or effective leadership.

But when the researcher looked at the number of calls the fundraisers placed the following week, he found that, compared with those who had not received a thank-you, those who had received the director's thanks ended up placing a lot more calls (63 versus 41). The simple act of demonstrating gratefulness for people's work had a major impact on the employees' work output.

Surprisingly, research shows that many managers are reticent to engage in these simple acts of kindness, worried about how they will be interpreted and received. Miscalibrated expectations and a failure to anticipate the positive impact can interfere in a leader's willingness to offer these acts of kindness in daily life. But the research also clearly shows that small acts of kindness are appreciated.

HOW TO IMPLEMENT SIMPLE GESTURES

I am delighted to be able to share with you, in the coming pages, a collection of small gestures that I have observed, used, and promoted over these many years. Small gestures like this—an invitation to join a meeting, an introduction on a call, and so on—are powerful. I can vouch for the fact that they can have a deep and meaningful impact on both parties, with the giver demonstrating thoughtful intention and the recipient feeling important.

Start with the Basics

At the most basic level, and perhaps this sounds old-fashioned, I'm talking about having "nice manners." Greeting people, thanking them, saying hello. These gestures are small but meaningful to people because they are about recognition and affirmation and human connection.

Christine Gregoire, former governor of the state of Washington, CEO of Challenge Seattle, and visionary leader of the greater Seattle region, shared the first powerful moment when she realized just how important it was to greet people:

> I had graduated from the University of Washington with a teaching certificate, but believe it or not, there were too many teachers at that time. I couldn't find a job, but I also couldn't tell my folks I was going to be unemployed. I ended up as a receptionist for my first eighteen months of employment. I did not think this would be much of a job, sitting at the desk, answering phones, saying hello, and directing those who walked in. But it became obvious to me, as the most "frontline" employee in that state office, how important each person is in an organization. As the first one anyone saw when they walked in the door and the last as they walked out, I was, without question, leaving an impression on each visitor to our office. Even in that job, with the first-line role, I was deserving of recognition in the state office for my role. And my initial greeting of each visitor was very important.

I would imagine that the idea of saying "thank you" does not need much advocacy from me, and there are many ways to give thanks.

Some people appreciate being called out publicly, so when you're in a large group gathering and you have a chance to thank those less tenured, in front of everyone, go for it! But thanking people in real time, one-on-one, with sincerity, can also be meaningful.

Do not underestimate the value of the tried-and-true written correspondence; any email or text will work to express your gratitude for those who helped you organize an event, accomplish a goal, or beat a sales forecast. When this is done outside the bounds of a performance review, it has significant value. Don't overthink it; I'm talking about a note of gratitude for going above and beyond or recognizing an all-nighter (no doubt one of many) that made a difference.

Be a Person First

You have a lot to do—numbers to hit, operations to oversee, strategies to develop. That is true, but you also do this with other people as part of a team. Small gestures can acknowledge the recipient in a very specific, intimate, and personal way.

Geraldine Rhodes shared two simple gestures that mean much to her. The first is when someone not only asks about her personal life but actually remembers things that are important to her, such as names of family members, hobbies, and vacations: "These gestures are a signal that someone wants to form a genuine relationship. Many of us spend so much time in our jobs, it's almost all-consuming. Feeling like people care makes the job sustainable and more fun."

She also appreciates when leaders check in after difficult world events, such as a massive natural disaster. "It shows that leaders care about more than just the work at hand. That's such a huge motivator."

Make the Most of Meetings

Bringing everyone in the room into the conversation is so important because that's how you achieve the collaboration you want out of the session. We've already looked at how we can ask insightful questions once the meeting is underway, but you can communicate respect and value to people with your actions in the following ways before the meeting even starts:

- Be on time. I have been told over and over the importance of this because we are all time-starved; that is not only a leader's problem. Being on time shows a huge level of respect for colleagues at every level in the organization. Conversely, if leaders are late, everyone in the room will assume that means they don't matter a whole heck of a lot to that person.
- Greet the newest or least tenured person in the room by name and ask a question about their weekend or something else personal.
- Introduce yourself to those you do not know, regardless of their level in the organization, and ask them to reciprocate and tell their names.
- Offer something personal about yourself, taking care to not use up too much airtime. The goal is to connect, make everyone feel they are full participants in the meeting, and help them get ready and willing to share.

Other small actions that convey meaning and value are refusing to cancel meetings with less tenured folks, jumping up and serving refreshments (Starbucks coffee, anyone?) as people or the refreshments arrive, and asking people how they pronounce their names if it's not obvious. Some may think it is taking a huge risk by asking this, but I have found that honoring people and showing interest far outweigh the risk of appearing insensitive.

Build a System

In addition to recognizing employees for a job well done, we can also recognize these human beings at a more personal level. You can honor people and show interest through notes, emails, texts, phone calls, announcements, or gifts. You can recognize people on their birthdays or when a new baby is born. As I noted earlier, you can go so far as sending handwritten, personalized holiday cards to everyone on your team. (Maybe a bit old-fashioned, but my experience is that the gesture and the effort are deeply appreciated, among young and old alike.)

To do this efficiently and equitably, you will need to build a system of recognition that works for you to execute, and this is a very tactical exercise. Calendars, notebooks, meeting notes, name-association techniques like saying someone's name out loud—use whatever works for you. While some of these ideas may take a bit more incremental time and process management, it's easy to develop a rhythm that will soon feel like second nature.

CALL TO ACTION

In the same way that small gestures can have a big impact, small changes in personal habits can lead to effective changes in process and overall behavior. Here are several ideas for how you can build small gestures into your regular routines.

Generate a List of Names

Whether you're planning to send out birthday greetings or recognize new team members in your regular meetings, you'll need to figure out who your audience is. And if you have a large team, you will also need to decide where to draw the line. When I came to the point of having more than a hundred people on my team, I was careful to include not only those I interacted with daily but also those who reported to many of my direct reports. I had a strong bias toward the folks at the more junior levels doing the day-to-day work supporting me. It was important to me—and, I believe, to them—for them to feel personally recognized, to feel valued by the leader, to feel seen. I also believed that if and when the going got tough and I needed their support, my ongoing recognition of them would benefit all of us.

CALL TO ACTION

Develop a list of all the people you want to remember from time to time so you won't need to scramble to remember when the time comes. You might rely on corporate communications for source data, such as when promotions are announced. You might also have separate lists for different occasions. For example, you might send birthday or holiday greetings to everyone in your department but only send notes of congratulations to your direct reports.

Create a Process

Recognizing employees can be time consuming, so having a clear process is critical. This is true whether you plan to send notes from your own desk or to deliver words of recognition in meetings where time is limited and agendas are full.

CALL TO ACTION

Once you've developed your list of names, indicate the method by which you plan to deliver your messages and the scheduled regularity. For recurring events like birthdays and holidays, add a task to your calendar—maybe even grouping them so that you send birthday greetings out just once per month to everyone celebrating that month. For those simple gestures you intend to deliver at meetings, be sure to set aside a specific allotment of time on the agenda and then track the time on your phone's stopwatch app. When time's up, it's up!

Craft Your Messages

My counsel: simple bullet points, in your words, from your heart. You do not have to write a novel! If you keep it simple for yourself, you are more likely to be successful in this endeavor.

Birthday notes: I was initially inspired by a former CEO of BCG who called every partner on their birthday. With 700 partners in the firm, this meant an average of two calls per day. When I took on leadership roles, I adopted an email process. Sometimes the message was as simple as a note in the subject line: *Happy birthday [name]! I hope you have a great day!! —Joe.* If they were a close friend, I might add many more exclamation points. If they were very close, I'd add a brief note in the body of the email and also send a text. Simple, I know, but as the numbers grew from the tens to hundreds to thousands as my roles expanded, I could not let myself freeze over the message.

Congratulations notes: Again, these can be simple notes just to let the employee know you're thinking of them and appreciating their work. It can be as simple as this:

Congratulations [name]:

Great stuff!! Really great for BCG, and great for you! So proud!!
Be well and enjoy,

—Joe

CALL TO ACTION

Develop a handful of prewritten messages to keep on hand and refer to when the time comes to send out your messages.

Build It into a Habit

Once you've created a process, it's easy to turn some of these practices—like sending birthday greetings or thank-you notes—into habits. It's especially helpful to create regular action items in your calendar or task lists to do these things at the beginning of the month, on the first day of the week, or even every day.

CALL TO ACTION

Some behaviors aren't process driven, and those can often be the more difficult ones to adopt. To really cement some of these into habit, you may want to remind yourself multiple times a day to practice the following:

- Make (even brief) eye contact and smile whenever walking into meetings.
- Greet others by their names or repeat their names when first introduced, and use their names again as you leave the meeting.
- Say "thank you"—a lot—and write immediate thank-you notes for unexpected support.
- Show up on time for meetings, or send a note even if you're going to be just a few minutes late.
- Resist the temptation to cancel on others, especially without adequate notice and strong reason.
- Acknowledge every person in the room, or on your video meetings, when you arrive.
- Introduce yourself to people you don't know and ask them to introduce themselves to you.

- Share something personal about yourself.
- Ask those who are less senior to share something about their lives in that moment.
- Ask people to pronounce their names if it is not obvious to you.
- Be the first up in a large meeting to hand out refreshments.

FINAL THOUGHTS

These acts require a small amount of effort but are acknowledging something important to the recipient—an emotional moment, an important event, something they feel proud of, something that was difficult for them. Even more powerful is when the effort and the small act are unexpected, either because of the personal nature of the acknowledgment or the hierarchy of roles; thus they become very memorable to the receiver. At a very basic level, particularly in our high-performing professional world, many of us are striving for the approval, the gold star, the pat on the back. As a result, all of these gestures that acknowledge another can create a bond between two people, can build loyalty, and can ultimately enhance team dynamics and performance.

They will be enhanced, too, when you help your team open their hearts by doing something that's admittedly very challenging on many dimensions: sharing about yourself. You can start by sharing photos of your family, talking about people who made a difference in your life, or taking time to share a professional failure—as we know, we often learn more from our mistakes than our successes. When you open your life, sharing both your feelings and your fears, you invite others to share theirs. You create a huge safe space, and in so doing, you free people to engage, to create, to take chances and explore.

8

BE VULNERABLE

Give Up the Mask

The old leadership model, and the corporate culture it created, dictated that our personal and professional lives did not overlap. Today we must be respectful of others' boundaries but also willing to be personally accessible. We need to be true to our real selves and willing to reveal our fears and challenges, which are often driven in part by our personal situations. This is probably the trickiest chapter to write but, in my view, one of the most important. Having the courage to share your fears and challenges is powerful and freehearted, and it is critical to building trust. As a leader, and in community with your colleagues, when you openheartedly cross that line (sharing more of your personal self, opportunities, challenges, uncertainties, and even insecurities and anxieties than you are typically comfortable doing), it offers freedom for others to do the same.

I tend to wear my emotions on my sleeve, and I have always liked sharing my personal life, so it's natural for me to be vulnerable in the workplace. Indeed, I have been known to cry in front of many people, in person and on Zoom. I even cried at age 23 through my wedding vows. The minister, a good friend and our college professor, had to walk me through the vows sentence by sentence. All the while, as my calm and collected spouse spoke her vows with clarity, strength, and love, my tears continued to flow.

A good friend once pointed out to me that it was easier for me than it would be for others: "Joe, it can be almost sweet when you cry. Not many will harshly judge a white male business leader in their sixties if they push the envelope." He was right: because of my race, gender, age, and position, it *is* much easier for me to share with impunity. I acknowledge that I face few repercussions when I reveal myself. Can the same be true for a 36-year-old woman of color, or even a 36-year-old white man? What about people of various gender identities, sexual orientations, races, religions, neurotypes, and abilities? While it may be difficult, or even frightening, for you to cross your own line, I encourage you to try. As the leader, it's up to you to be the first to unpack the benefits of letting go of your shadows, facing your fears, and making authentic connections.

VULNERABILITY CAN BE LIBERATING

It wasn't always easy for me. My parents split in 1965, when I was eight. I recall the evening I found out: we were at my grandparents' wheat farm in eastern Washington, and as I was going to sleep one night, I asked my mom when we were going home to see my dad.

She answered plainly: "Joey, we will not be going home to live with your dad." Of course, as an eight-year-old I didn't understand why not. I didn't understand that my dad was gay.

In fact, I would not realize this for years. I would go down to the Bay Area in California to visit him for a week or two each year, and his sexual orientation simply didn't cross my mind. Even as the years went by and the signs should have become more obvious during these visits, I still missed it—or, probably, I subconsciously chose not to see the truth. You might imagine the questions I refused to let bubble to the surface of my mind: *If he is gay, how am I here? Did he ever like my mom? Why did they get married? Did my mom know? Why is he gay?* And on and on.

I finally acknowledged it in 1991, when my dad visited me in Australia. He had a line of pill bottles on the bathroom counter, and although I had no idea what they were, my wife, Sarah, knew. She had been a nurse who worked with the San Francisco gay community during the AIDS crisis. We asked him about the bottles, and everything at that point became abundantly clear. Still, after that conversation, I did not speak of it much (perhaps not at all) except with my two brothers, on rare occasions.

After my dad died, in 1997, I began to grow more comfortable with the idea that he was gay and to be open about it with people in one-on-one settings. Over time, I actually became a bit proud that my dad chose to live the life he was meant to live, even having a "roommate" for 25 years, until they both died of AIDS complications. But I still wasn't willing to cross my line and share this information broadly, until I was leading BCG North America. It was 2017 when I decided to take a chance.

As part of its commitment to diversity, equity, and inclusion, BCG had established multiple diversity networks to support employees regarding gender and LGBTQ+ identity as well as challenges relating to race, ethnicity, disability, military veteran status, and other dimensions. In my role as North America chair, I typically joined each diversity network's annual conference to share a few words, recognize accomplishments and continued challenges, and reinforce my support of these networks. The gay/lesbian network, BCG's first diversity network, was a tight-knit group of people who always had each other's back and did all they could to be true action allies. They took each other's success very seriously, and this was the network where I crossed my line.

Why did I decide to share then? I knew that being honest and open and sharing vulnerabilities were important and powerful leadership characteristics, and I thought sharing would better connect me to this group of colleagues—a set of colleagues with whom, at least in my mind, I shared a small bit of community. Yet I also knew this was not a moment to be taken lightly. I had to be very thoughtful to not come across as claiming to know their lived experience—I did not, and I cannot. I needed to ensure the group knew I was sincere in sharing; I wasn't just looking for acceptance but instead wanted to communicate that I had some level of connection with their lives. I wrote this speech carefully. I got counsel: "Be sincere, Joe; be honest. Tell us as you; be real. Share your uncertainty—about sharing with us and about how you felt about your dad being gay. Do not be afraid to let flow whatever emotion comes." I practiced.

I did not use notes. I stood in front of several hundred BCGers in a Chicago office conference room. Nervous, I wondered, *Will I get this out? Will I break down? How will it come across?*

"I know I do not know your life," I began, "or what you go through day by day, but I have a bit of a connection. My dad was gay, and he died of complications from AIDS."

I did it. I got it out. But as I went on, my mind worried about what they thought: *Who do you think you are to tell us this, to pretend to share in a portion of our lived experience? Why are you telling us this—do you want some sort of empathy, sympathy, support? Is this about you, or all of us?*

As it turned out, my fears were off base. The crowd's reaction was first surprise, then warm acceptance. The moment for me was very liberating.

Why? In work, we typically try to deal with most situations in an unemotional, rational way. When topics become emotional, they are far more challenging—maybe even confusing or embarrassing—to discuss. My values had developed in a time—the 1960s and 1970s—

when, to be frank, being gay was not generally accepted or seen as "normal" in most communities. Although my understanding of humanity evolved as the years went by, and I grew to accept and embrace differences, I still struggled emotionally with my dad's life, and it remained disconcerting for me to have been the son of a (seemingly) happily married gay man. My way to deal with those emotions had been to bury them. To remain silent.

When I finally revealed the story of my dad, in front of that large group—an admittedly safe audience who would understand more than others might—I was publicly accepting what had been buried. I was putting it out in the open. I had, years before, accepted my dad being gay, but with that open conversation in 2017, I was finally embracing it. I was moving past my outdated values, formed decades earlier, and coming to a place where I could finally, and with compassion, embrace the history of my childhood, my dad's struggles, and my dad's life.

While I had always been a bit more vulnerable than most (recall my vows at 23 years old), this Chicago experience was powerful. It moved me even further across my own line. It opened me even more to sharing my own uncertainties when I was lost regarding a work problem and thus needed to ask for help. It brought me even closer to my day-to-day team, who was with me in Chicago, as they saw that I was willing to share and engage in a personal and vulnerable way, thereby freeing them to do the same. It also brought me closer to members of the Pride@BCG network. To this day, I will run into people who were at that session who thank me for sharing but also, more importantly, thank me for signaling that BCG is an open, caring culture that is willing to share vulnerabilities as well as be supportive of all backgrounds and personal situations. An obvious benefit for me, too, has been that people at all levels in BCG have since been willing to come up to me to share, to engage, or to challenge what I or the company might be doing while knowing, I believe, that I will be open enough to listen with minimal judgment.

This experience and others have taught me that when you share your authentic self, this freeheartedness offers a special kind of accessibility, one that resonates. It says to another person, "I trust YOU, and I'm willing to share this intimate part of myself before I ask anything of you. I'm willing to go first." And taking the first step in this human connection has positive effects:

- it builds lasting trust;
- it builds a sense of emotional safety;
- it makes space for others to be real and vulnerable.

Like all the generous acts, the secondary benefits are not the drivers, but they are bountiful nonetheless. This freeheartedness allows you to be more yourself at work. It creates closer community. It removes the roadblocks of roles and hierarchy, giving people permission to be multidimensional at work. It makes room for people to feel safe in collaboration, and that makes them more confident, creative, and productive.

THE CHALLENGE: LETTING GO

Sharing fears is not cool. As leaders, we do not want to appear weak. Have you ever found yourself on the edge of a deeply personal, emotional reaction at work, whether in front of a few or many, and felt yourself shutting down? Do any of these reasons for holding back sound familiar to you?

- I must not share those emotions; this is business.
- I keep my authentic self at home.

- If I appear vulnerable, I will look weak.
- My vulnerability can be used against me.
- What will my boss think? My colleagues? Will any of them use this to push me aside?
- I don't know how to speak from my heart.
- Given who I am, I cannot let my vulnerabilities show.
- I don't know where to draw the line, what is appropriate to bring to work, or what might be accepted and influential from me.

Being a leader isn't easy. We face problems every day in research and development, sales and marketing, operations, finances, human resources, and many other arenas. But we usually know how to amass our resources and develop solutions. So it's hard to imagine that just talking about one's own experiences, or even one's own inability to have an answer here and now about a corporate challenge, could be so difficult and prompt a disproportionate amount of angst for many of us—angst that hides the true benefits of being willing to let go.

THE RESEARCH: BENEFITS OF CONNECTING BY SHARING YOURSELF

The prevailing belief in leadership has for years been that emotions undermine good decision-making and other cognitive tasks. There is no room in the workplace for emotions. But new research is very clear: by repressing emotions, we greatly inhibit human functioning. Moreover, when we bring them into the workplace, in their many forms, we inspire our teams to perform at their best.

According to research conducted by HeartMath Institute, the organizations that will endure and even thrive will be those that reject flat-earth attitudes about heart and leadership and that accept how feelings and emotions play an enormous role in driving employee behavior.[1] According to director of research Rollin McCraty, "It's our emotions that drive our biochemistry—not the other way around. Feelings and emotions, therefore, determine our level of engagement in life, what motivates us, and what we care about."

As Scott Kirby noted, and as I have also heard from other CEOs, there is often a fear in leadership about being transparent, about having the courage to tell bad news, about indirectly admitting that you personally, as the leader, do not have the solutions or a clear path to the answer. The Potential Project studied the issue of transparency and found that, when leaders have the courage to be transparent, amazing things happen:[2]

- employee job satisfaction improves by 86 percent;
- employee engagement grows by 53 percent;
- organizational commitment grows by 61 percent;
- satisfaction with the leader increases by 77 percent.

Your teams are looking to you for honesty and transparency. It builds confidence.

In a 2018 study on vulnerability in leadership, Stephanie Lopez found that leaders who demonstrate courage by confronting their own fears and uncertainties head-on are more likely to lean into vulnerability with those they lead and to demonstrate transparency and an openness to emotional exposure.[3]

Mary Kay Copeland from St. John Fisher University conducted a study in 2016 looking at the relationship between authenticity and leadership effectiveness. Authenticity was defined as "accepting and acknowledging one's thoughts, emotions, needs, wants, preferences, or beliefs and acting consistently with those beliefs and with one's inner person."[4] An authentic leader confidently conveys their beliefs in speech and action. The study concluded, unsurprisingly, that authenticity can incrementally improve the positive outcomes of a leader.

Emma Seppälä, in the *Harvard Business Review* article "What Bosses Gain by Being Vulnerable," cites multiple behavioral studies on the importance of authenticity and vulnerability to building connection and trust.[5] If you "embrace an authentic and vulnerable stance: Your staff will see you as a human being; they may feel closer to you; they may be prompted to share advice; and—if you are attached to hierarchy—you may find that your team begins to feel more horizontal." She also notes that inauthenticity backfires: "While we may try to appear perfect, strong or intelligent in order to be respected by others, pretense often has the opposite effect intended." Research by Paula Niedenthal, professor of psychology at the University of Wisconsin–Madison, working with Sebastian Korb, supports Seppälä's observation.[6] Seppälä notes that Niedenthal's research indicates "we resonate too deeply with one another to ignore inauthenticity."

My experience has been the same across my work career. Those who are "too perfect" simply do not connect as well, and, in my observation, eventually the organizational climb for them comes to an end—the speed of which depends on their "level" of inauthenticity. Unlike those who are able to "be more real," those who are "too perfect" fail to build connections that motivate and inspire.

Seppälä also cites an interesting exercise on the emotional power of sharing: "Johann Berlin, CEO of Transformational Leadership for Excellence, recounts an experience he had while teaching a workshop in a Fortune 100 company. The participants were all higher-level management. After an exercise in which pairs of participants shared an event from their life with each other, one of the top executive managers approached Johann. Visibly moved by the experience, he said 'I've worked with my colleague for over 25 years and have never known about the difficult times in his life.'"

This set of leaders had not even found a way to share their important personal moments with one another, let alone with their staff. But, as was noted, the sharing brought out a deeper humanity. Imagine the power and benefits if this set of leaders went the next step and repeated the exercise with members of their staff.

HOW TO SHARE BY STEPPING FURTHER ACROSS YOUR LINE

I talked with a handful of good friends and colleagues about crossing lines, both professionally and personally. Some of their stories, and some more of mine, are shared here.

Go First

Brian Gross said it's really quite simple: "You should never expect more from others than you give." He also said that, when I was willing to cry on occasion in front of so many at BCG, it opened up many people. "You were willing to set the line way over, you gave others permission. What they came to believe was *Joe will listen, and I can share my struggles.*"

You may believe it is "right" to always be strong and in charge, but I do not share that belief; it is not my experience, and data do not support that view. As the leader, it's up to you to open the door to sharing vulnerabilities. People want to bring their whole self safely to work, to ask for help when they are stuck, to be able to admit they do not know it all. You can help them, not only as a caring leader who listens and engages but as an authentic, open, vulnerable, and honest leader. If you share some of your challenges, fears, feelings, and worries, you free your people to do the same. But you must go first. You must be the role model.

Be Real

The value of honesty is, of course, a given, and it's especially powerful when you acknowledge your uncertainties. If you want to crack the toughest problems, you need to know the toughest roadblocks and uncover ways around those roadblocks. You need from your teams their most radical, creative ideas. Sharing roadblocks with your teams can be scary for many; no one wants to be the one who exposes weaknesses—their own or the organization's. The more honest you are about the challenges your organization faces, the more others will share what they see with you . . . and the faster you'll get to the best answer and deliver the most lasting result.

In April 2020, I held my second all–North America staff town hall to address the COVID-19 situation as we were beginning to close offices. It was an emotionally powerful town hall, at a time when all of us were still wondering what the potential health threat of COVID might be, where our work lives were heading, and how we would operate in a lockdown world. This was my first Zoom town hall, with no professional film crew. My first town hall had been from an "empty" BCG Washington, DC, office, filmed live and webcast to the entire North America staff.

For this first Zoom meeting, I spoke from my daughter's childhood bedroom, untouched in the many years since she had moved out; she was now in her own home, with three wonderful children and number four on the way. The room was painted light blue with puffy white clouds, and in the background, people could see the walls and her dressing table and whimsical mirror above.

I had already established the habit of moving around day by day to different rooms in our home, accustomed to traveling three to five days a week for over 20 years before the pandemic. I figured I would satisfy my need for a change of scenery by moving rooms. On this day, I landed in her room. I wish I could say it was intentional or that I understood in advance the power of this room. Perhaps there was some instinct deep down that knew it could drive an impression.

I started by expressing my empathy for everyone, acknowledging that we were all going through a lot at that point in time, in our own ways, and that the virus was hitting especially hard for some. Then I shared my own situation.

I struggled through the words as I spoke, thinking of my family—and, in my mind and heart, also thinking of my colleagues and their families. My throat tightened; my voice cracked. I had to pause several times as the trembling grew, and I worked to avoid the tears flowing. I told my staff,

> It was difficult when Sarah and I put our oldest daughter and our four-month-old granddaughter on a plane home to Germany ten days ago as international borders were closing and airlines were cutting international flights. And then it was even more troubling when we received a text from her the next day letting us know that our son-in-law had just tested positive for COVID-19. Meanwhile, another of our daughters is a nurse in Seattle at Harborview Medical Center. While we are extremely proud of her, I do have to admit there is some anxiety given that she's exposed to the virus every day she goes to work.

The reactions to my honesty, to sharing my personal fears, were touching. One mother of three children—and grandmother of five—sent an email to say how moved she was when I talked about my family, and she assured me we were in her prayers. Another email I received was both affirming and surprising.

Subject: Power in words

Joe,

Thank you for your inspiring words today. Not only did they uplift my spirit, but they also reminded me we are truly better together. Thank you.

PS: I loved that you spoke from a room with clouds on the wall. It's the humanity in all of this that brings me to tears.

Her reaction to the clouds was a surprise and was reinforced by other messages posted on Fishbowl (an anonymous app used by many in professional services businesses), such as one that read,

"Really loving the wallpaper in whatever room Joe Davis is in. It's almost like being outside" (72 likes)
It's Hannah's room
I love it
The heart mirror is an adorable accent.
Especially as he chokes up 😊

As I hope you can sense and feel, these genuine invitations into my own personal experiences invited unexpected, and welcome, emotional responses. It appeared that people no longer saw me only as this 35-year veteran, very senior manager "way above them" but also as a person struggling with fears and uncertainty. They shared with me more about themselves after that, through email, Zoom meetings, and phone calls—more personally and more honestly. This in turn opened more heartfelt conversations across our North America team. I was also told that my heartfelt message made people feel more a part of our supportive community and that it gave them more confidence we would get through the uncertainty together. It was an important lesson for me on the benefits of sharing one's own vulnerabilities honestly.

Be Humble

"I do not know."

Such a simple phrase, and, in fact, a very safe phrase. But so many leaders will not admit they do not know. They won't show that they don't have the answers. And that is simply backward. When you act like you know it all, what are you modeling? That your colleagues should know it all, or at least not admit when they don't? Think about how much time is wasted and how much thinking is held back if someone keeps charging forward trying to do what they guess is best when they simply don't know.

This is yours to fix. When you tell others you do not know, it's more than just listening to learn, as we explored earlier. It's also about encouraging others to open up to you; they are more willing to admit when *they* don't know, and now you are working together to solve the issue. Also, when you don't pretend to know it all, you allow others to share what they do know. You create a productive environment of safe and open communication.

Ian Pancham spoke with me about his journey crossing his line:

I have spent most of my life working to reduce my vulnerabilities and taking a defensive posture. When I started to expose myself more, in the context of "I do not know" as a less-tenured person, I would always put it in the context of the specific topic or question, never showing that I might be a bit lost.

But as I stepped into leadership roles, I began to see a problem with this, on so many levels. First, I saw that people were expecting too much of themselves, trying to be more than they might be at that moment and pretending to know more than they did. This was unhealthy, and I needed a way to convince my teams that you don't always have to have all the answers yet.

Second, I found that we were hurting progress, and not getting the results we might have, because I wouldn't admit what I didn't know. This led people to hold back and not admit they were stuck or lost, and thus they'd make little progress. But when I exposed the truth—that I did not know—I was able to free them and to keep us all moving forward.

Finally, I found people assumed I knew more than I did because I hadn't admitted that I was also lost, and they'd come to me for answers, and that didn't help because now I had to explain that I didn't.

I have started crossing my line into exposing vulnerabilities with a simple "I do not know." It's been hard, and it's still hard, but I am still learning, experimenting, and taking chances.

While at Shell, Christina Sistrunk was overseeing rigs and off-shore facilities when they came to a point where they were not delivering adequate safety results:

> I had one contractor who was achieving a better safety record than our Shell team, and I asked if I could speak with him about his safety record. This may sound like a simple idea, but it was a giant step. I worked for a major oil company, and we simply did not call contractors and ask for help. Yep, it was corporate arrogance.
>
> If my colleagues had learned of my visit, they would have thought I was nuts—"Corporate-oil-America, and as a woman!" But I had to make a difference on safety, and to do that I had to accept some vulnerability. The contractor shared some of their tips, which we quickly implemented. Crossing my line was sure worth it for all of us.

Watch and Learn

We each must find our own ways to share vulnerabilities, step out of our comfort zone, and push past our lines. Think about a time when you saw another leader, or someone you deeply respect, open up and share their worries. How did you feel? Did it touch you, warm you to them, or give you a sense they were opening up—or even giving—a piece of themselves to you? Did it make you want to follow them even further? Did it free *you* even a tiny bit?

Capture those moments and recall the feeling of connection and trust you experienced when witnessing somebody else's vulnerability, and then use those moments as a springboard for changes in your own behavior and thought patterns. Stretch your perspective as you would stretch your muscles in the gym, seeking to look past your title and your role so that you can build deeper connections, warmth, and trust.

Christina agreed that it can be valuable to watch and learn from others: "If you have people around you courageous enough to be vulnerable: watch, watch, watch. Think deeply about how their actions would work for you, what it would feel like, and whether they would be consistent with who you are. Of course, you can't simply cut and paste another person's approach; people will judge you, and you must be consistent with who you are. But you can watch, learn, and experiment as you work to push your own envelope."

CALL TO ACTION

Just as this chapter was tricky to write, as I shared more of my own vulnerability, trying to come up with simple actions to help you cross and move your line is also tricky. Hopefully, the stories of my colleagues and my own experiences will inspire you.

Follow the Leaders

I suggest you start by reflecting on these stories and other examples where you have seen friends or colleagues crossing their own lines. What did you observe? What did they say or do to reveal their vulnerability? How did others react? What was the result? How might some of these other examples inspire you?

Susan Grimbilas was inspired by one of her colleagues who always had photographs of her family in the office despite conventional wisdom back then that women should maintain a strict dividing line between their personal and professional lives. The same colleague kept her calendar honest and transparent. For example, if she had to leave work to see her kid's play at school, the calendar showed "Sam's play" and not "personal appointment." "These were small things, but they signaled to the rest of us the importance of not hiding who you were or what you were doing. For people who might not be able to cry in front of others, or tell soul-revealing stories, it seems an easy first step to have your calendar show what you are doing."

Early in her career, Kedra Newsom worked in an environment of mainly white men and had modified her behavior to try to fit in. She lowered her voice and was always careful about what she said and how she said it. "But that took way too much brain space to be another," she said. "It was incredibly taxing and such a waste of time, and I didn't have the time to spend it not being me."

Later, she began to watch what some of her mentors did, and she sometimes questioned one about choices he'd made. He said he knew it was risky, but he didn't care. By the time she had children, she only had time to be herself, and ultimately, she came to believe that once you decide to share your true self, people want to be around you, and are inspired by you, thereby being able to do so much more. As she put it, "Once you decide to be more authentic, to be more vulnerable—there are massive benefits. The selfish benefit of it is very powerful. You attract great people. As you open up, your teams feel safer—and they bloom with their own potential. You simply win in so many ways—the upside is unlimited."

CALL TO ACTION

Take a look at your calendar. How are your personal commitments reflected? Then think about some recent conversations you've had with colleagues. What have you shared about your personal life? Are there joys or issues you wished you'd shared? How might you open up going forward?

Release Your Fears

As you assess how and when to reveal your vulnerabilities—and as the fear of doing so bubbles up—accept that fear. There are likely many times in the past when you've taken other scary chances and they worked out. Acknowledging this can help you give yourself permission to face current fears and take further chances. To test. To experiment.

Brian Gross put it this way: "Dial into your darkest spots, a moment that made you most sad in life. Go there, tiptoe in, realize you made it through. Realize life is too short, it does not matter, let me be me. I made it through that moment, and now I can be free."

A very funny story for me occurred in my mid-20s. I decided to take up the piano many years after the typical couple of years of intermittent lessons when I was 10 years old or so. I was basically a beginner. I will never forget my "first" recital. Here was 25-year-old me in a room full of 10-year-olds, their parents, and my wife, quite worried that I would be outshone by the children. I was at the piano. I started out. I was shaking, surprisingly nervous. As I reticently struck the piano keys, one by one, I heard one of the 10-year-old students say, "Mommy, he is really nervous." I am sure my one-by-one pluck-ing slowed even further. Ugh! *Now what—do I continue?* I did my best to put it aside and finish my simple piece.

I sure felt vulnerable at that moment, even though, admittedly, the stakes were not that high. It is, however, a wonderful reminder to me: it is OK to take a chance on a personal front.

CALL TO ACTION

Reflect back on a dark time and place for you, recalling how scared and nervous you were. Recall, too, how you found the courage to overcome that moment and survive—or even thrive. How did you make it through? How are you doing now? Did it hurt that much? Now think about how vulnerability frightens you today, and release those fears by envisioning how painful it will—or won't—be and how you might overcome it and even be in a better place once you've crossed that line.

Experiment

Any new endeavor requires practice, and learning how to become vulnerable is no different. "Be ready for that step when the moment comes," Brian Gross said. "When the opportunity presents itself, you are going to have to take a chance to reveal yourself, to be vulnerable. Take little steps, with small groups. It does not require a dramatic reveal."

I had an opportunity as I was starting to lead BCG's West Coast System. All the officers had recently received our year-end 360-degree feedback. I needed to connect with my new officer team. I needed them to open up on their challenges and opportunities if we were going to move the West Coast forward. In one of my first all-officer meetings, I decided to push myself over my line a bit and model by sharing to the entire group *my* year-end feedback—both the positive and the criticisms, including the work I had to do. I will say, many were stunned. They came up to me to tell me they were quite surprised by my move, but they also started to open up to me about where they needed help.

CALL TO ACTION

You can start with some safe chances when the stakes are not too high. Sit down with a teammate over coffee and tell them a bit about yourself, sharing a personal story or perspective. Go on a walk and talk about some of your challenges at that moment. Regardless of the venue, carve out some time to tell them about your family challenges at home and ask them about theirs (without probing) to open the connection.

While you can't always anticipate when the right time will arise, you can try to at least create space for practice and experimentation:

- Reflect on this past week and ask yourself how you might constructively respond to criticism you received or admit a mistake you made.
- As you plan next week's agenda, find an opportunity when you might take a stand on an unpopular perspective.
- Looking out into the next month, identify which upcoming meetings or events will set up opportunities for you to take a small step across your line.

After experimenting in each of these moments, set aside some time for reflection. How did it feel? How did your colleagues react to you? Can you go further?

Try "I Don't Know"

Your humility gives permission for you to not be perfect, and it also makes room for another's success. And yet it's so hard to practice!

I recall a powerful experience in my early 30s. I was a new project leader. I was trying to do an analysis, and I did not know the math. I was stuck. I would not be able to help my team as I was expected to; we could fall behind. Knowing loss of time was my biggest enemy, I took a chance. I walked down the hall to my partner on that project and told him, with trepidation, that I was stuck, as I did not know how to do this particular math. Would he nicely say I should know how to do this? Would he privately think I was a dummy? Would he wonder if I could do this job? Was I jeopardizing my career? His response: "Hmm, I am not sure how to do that either. Let's go ask Phil; I am sure he will know." Wow! I took a chance and was not chastised. More importantly, he did not pretend he was too busy, send me away, and then privately find the answer and bring it back to me. Rather, he powerfully shared his simple vulnerability with me. I have never forgotten that moment.

CALL TO ACTION

The next time you're with your team and you don't really know the answer to a problem—or you don't know it yet—challenge yourself by saying aloud, "I don't know."

Then take a moment to process what happened, whether on the spot with your team or later in the day through private reflection. What happened? Did it hurt? Did admitting you didn't have the answer set you back? Or did it open others up, promoting even more engagement and exploration?

Make It Safe

When you share yourself, you sometimes need to start small. Brian Gross cautioned that "big, dramatic reveals" can be too much for you *and* for your audience. When you cross your line slowly, gently, and effectively, you're also modeling for others how to do this. And just as *you* begin to practice how to be more authentic and vulnerable, you can encourage others to do the same, as long as you've created a safe space for them by inviting them to share, first in one-on-one sessions with you and later in small group settings.

CALL TO ACTION

As you plan your next regular team meeting, set aside some practice time for crossing lines. Let the team know why this is important to do and establish ground rules, such as respect and confidentiality, to create a safe environment. Assure everyone that this is an experiment, an opportunity to practice, and then be the first one to reveal something personal, paving the way for others to open up.

FINAL THOUGHTS

Brian shared some of his wisdom from his own practice of generous and heartfelt sharing:

> For me in the early days, the line on transparency (about being gay) was hard; I was not close with anyone—Mom, Dad. I never shared.
>
> I stayed in the closet for years. I avoided the opportunity to explain who I was, to be me. I was always playacting, trying to show what was expected.

I will say, this limited my ability to connect wholly with work colleagues (and others, of course). If you want to hear others' challenges, you must share yours. It is not a one-way street; you will not get authentic answers unless you want the authentic truth. If you want to hear the problems, the challenges, you must be willing to hear them, and you must open the path for them.

This can be quite important in life, but also in business. If you lose too many opportunities to be open with people, to be authentic, then they will believe you do not really care, you are not going to share, and thus you are not going to hear their problems. If you get to this point, you lose the opportunity to know where people stand, where your organization sits, where the skeptics are, and what the obstacles are that need to be uncovered and addressed to make real progress.

When you cross your line, sharing your challenges and your uncertainties, you are giving of yourself, you are leveling the playing field and making it safe for you to be just two people sharing, two people in conversation. You are making it safe to be imperfect. You are building an environment of honesty and respect that is inspiring, freeing, and empowering.

This book is an exploration of generosity within your business practice. These acts are based on respect, advocacy, humility, honor, honesty, and attentiveness. All of this is within you—I'm certain you use elements daily. To transform your leadership, you must identify specific ways in which you can elevate these actions to the surface, to bring, with intention, this multidimensionality to your already exceptional results-driven skill set. But where to start? We are all works in progress. Let me share some ideas to build your heart-led leadership.

9

CHANGE YOURSELF

Be Generous in Your Own
Personal Growth

We can all be the change we want to be. We can strive to live our personal and work lives in wonderful harmony. By bringing together the skills that we have explored through this book and making them a practice in our daily work lives, we can each build a better self.

And with a better self as your foundation, you can develop, and inspire your employees and your team, ultimately supporting all as they perform as their best selves, with all the commensurate benefits. And, as we've explored, the work world is yearning for a shift in leadership styles and workplace culture. Employees want to be seen as more than people who accomplish objectives—rather, as whole individuals. And they want to work with you to contribute to a better world—one that is larger than you, the people on your team, or your organization overall.

But how do you craft your own path forward to incorporate this new work into your life? And when?

A DAUNTING TASK

When Christine Gregoire was reelected as the Washington State governor in 2008, she had to apply some of these concepts while making sure everyone had a seat at the table.

I had to cut $11 billion out of a $37-billion budget as the great financial crisis was hitting. That sounds hard enough, but as you likely know, there are many budget lines at the state level that are mandated by federal law or the constitution, so our pool of available funds to cut was not really $37 billion. This was one heck of an exercise.

The typical process in this situation would be for the governor to set some broad targets for each state agency and then bring in the head of each agency to talk about what they are planning to cut. But with the daunting task in front of us, I wasn't comfortable with that approach. I decided to take a two-step inclusive approach, even though I was sure that hadn't ever been done in Washington State—and I'm not sure it was done in many, if any, other states.

Our first step was to engage the public. We held town halls across the state, which turned out to be well attended, to walk through the budget, describe the cuts that were required, and the type of options we had. What we sought at this level was input and engagement—not buy-ins.

The second step was the more unusual, and it was the action that yielded huge benefits. I gathered all the agency heads into one room, and we spent hours and hours, together, going through, agency by agency, where we might cut. I had each agency head describe the cuts contemplated, and then as a team we probed and pushed on the implications of those cuts, identifying the pain they would likely yield for the agencies, for the state, and for the citizens.

I remember one example where the head of human services said we could cut the podiatry benefit out of state medical funding. Someone asked what that would mean: "If someone had serious foot damage, and maybe needed a serious operation to save their foot, we could not provide it, and they would likely lose their foot."

Wow, illustrations like that one were powerful. It opened all of us to listen to one another, to think beyond our own "fiefdoms," and to figure out how to share the pain in a way that was best for the state and the citizens rather than to simply try to "protect" individual agencies. Each of us also learned so much about the other agencies and challenges, which eliminated complaints of *What about me?*

The collaboration and inclusive connection were awesome. We were all in this together, and, interestingly, when it came time to testify at the state legislature about the cuts, there was none of the typical whining, *my department had to do this*, to generate sympathy from the legislators and maybe save some of their agencies money. Rather, we all looked hard—together—at what we needed to do. We all made tough decisions. We all shared in the pain we thought was needed and came up with a unified state plan.

Going forward, we had a strongly inclusive team, and when other tough challenges came up, we rapidly banded together to solve them effectively, far better than I could have imagined. All were sympathetic to the role of others; we had much more focus on *we* than *me*.

As I listened to Christine tell this story, I heard so many aspects of leading from the heart. She began with a place of humility and collaboration. She created many inclusionary tables. Everyone was curious about each other's expertise and listened to learn. The result was a team that was aligned and willing to make tough calls, and that in turn created a new culture that generated creative ideas to get the job done.

THE CHALLENGE: GETTING STARTED

You may be thinking, *OK, I hear you; my role as leader is even more important than I was thinking, but, wow, there is a lot here to get after. Where do I start?*

As a leader, you're used to making your own decisions and choosing your own path. But what we're talking about here isn't the more typical left-brained, analytical decision. You may in fact be embarking on a journey that will exercise your right brain, your intuition, and other parts of yourself that feel foreign in some ways.

HOW TO MAKE CHANGES: AN ILLUSTRATION THROUGH ONE OF MY PERSONAL JOURNEYS

Setting aside some of your old ways of doing things and shaking things up to implement some of the new practices we've been discussing can be overwhelming. The first thing you need to do is get out of your own way. You've got to avoid falling victim to analysis paralysis as you try to figure out what to do and recognize that, sometimes, opportunities present themselves seemingly of their own volition. You may not be happy with the path presented, but often it's the right one.

When I moved to the Bay Area to lead the West Coast System, BCG's business had been steady, and I was tasked with growing it. There was much to be done, and I put in place many leadership and management basics. My team developed a vision of doubling the business in four years, and we called this initiative the Road to 200 ($200 million revenue). We set clear people-growth plans, prioritized clients, established metrics, and carefully tracked our progress.

This was also a perfect opportunity to put into practice many of the concepts that I've since written about in this book. For example, I spent the first three months listening carefully. I knew there was a lot I didn't know, and I met personally with every managing director and partner, each manager, each business-services leader, and the finance team. I listened to their challenges, their views of opportunities, and where they thought I could be most effective. One person gave me a powerful insight: "Do not let anyone tell you the market is tough; we just have to up our own confidence and boldness, and then we can grow."

I also worked to connect personally with as many as I could throughout the West Coast offices. My wife and I flew to each office to have dinner with the partners and managers, as well as their spouses or partners. We also energized the summer family weekend, a BCG tradition to bring together all BCG members from a particular office, along with their families, to connect, share, get to know one another, and simply have fun. Over my years at BCG, this tradition has created incredible bonding experiences—among BCGers and between the employees and BCG overall. For many years, my young children could tell you each family-weekend location and with whom we shared rooms. The West Coast also had this tradition but had not been able to muster the energy and positivity to build the wonderful bonds. My goal was to rekindle the energy and spirit of these weekends, and I asked each of my grown children to attend in order to help me share a bit more of my personal life with my new colleagues.

Authenticity and honesty were also key to my efforts. As mentioned earlier, I once shared my personal 360-degree officer feedback with the officer team. On another occasion, we were in an office-leadership annual staff review meeting, speaking about the placement of an individual in our rankings system. Many were afraid to rank this person as they should be ranked; even though it was a "fine spot," they interpreted it as a kiss of death. I stopped the conversation and said, "I was in that placement for much of my career and I did OK, so let's do what is right."

The immediate response was silence and awkwardness; people were stunned. There I was, the head of the office system, admitting to those reporting to me—even though I did not need to reveal this information—that I had been ranked "average" for years. I was told that these examples of honesty ultimately served to open up the leadership team with each other and the staff.

I also lived up to my own belief in candid feedback at the individual level. For example, an officer who was underperforming reached out to me and acknowledged that he didn't think he was performing as well as he should have been. "I expect this will be a tough year-end review cycle for me," he said. "Do you mind if I start looking for a new job now [midsummer] and gracefully leave BCG in the new year before the review cycle finishes and I am undoubtedly outplaced?" My response? "Yes, you are not meeting expectations, and yes, you can leave BCG gracefully of your own accord."

Creating an atmosphere of inclusivity was also high on my priority list, and I looked for multiple opportunities to invite more people to the table to participate in our efforts toward aspiration setting, planning, and monitoring. I implemented new officer and manager monthly meetings and officer, manager, and project leader quarterly meetings. These larger, more inclusive leadership meetings had not been done before. I also formed a new West Coast management team consisting of officer and practice-area leaders, our business-services (support) team, and our finance team.

I recognized talent and pushed employees to team and contribute wherever they were able. When I had first arrived, people with deep functional expertise, such as supply chain knowledge, remained focused only on the clients in the industry to which they were assigned, even if they were not busy and even when their functional expertise was needed to serve clients in other industries. There were hard (artificial) silos on the West Coast blocking more effective teaming, and I brought down those walls immediately.

Although the concept of being an action ally wasn't quite on my radar yet, I still acted as one. For example, a junior finance person, who worked indirectly for me, was very talented but seemingly scared to death. I invited her personally into reviews with me and encouraged her to share her work and engage. I pushed her pretty hard, even when she was reticent. As a result, her confidence visibly increased in leadership meetings, and she went on to earn two promotions and then get promoted into a different functional area—one in which she was inexperienced but now had the confidence to take on.

Finally, I pushed myself on the small gestures, working to up my game. For example, I decided to recognize every West Coast staff person's birthday and to send each of them a handwritten holiday card. It was a lot of cards, but the connection I personally built with the West Coast employees was palpable.

We surpassed the aspirational goal, growing to a $250 million revenue in three years. There are many reasons for the success, but people have told me that three stuck out the most to them: We took teaming to a whole new level. We recognized and grew the talent. And we built confidence—first that of the leaders and then that of the entire team. I like to say we unleashed an already talented group of people to become the best they could be.

Then, for the last two years of my role as chair of BCG North America, I led the firm through the pandemic, the most intense

experience in our lifetime, and these responsibilities led to connections with my teams in ways I could never have imagined. It required
complete vulnerability, compassion, and careful listening. It also required firm decision-making. It was at times gut-wrenching to
learn of others' uncertainties and fears and their hardships in an impersonal work-from-home model; exhausting to always be on and
upbeat yet realistic; and disappointing when I was not able to give
people everything they thought they needed. Yet it was the most
satisfying and exhilarating time of my professional life.

And now I have found myself on another new path, yet again
working to implement the practices we've been discussing. I am definitely a work in progress.

I am still vulnerable: Once the time came to hand over the reins,
I wondered, *Now what?* I would continue to love leading. I would
continue to love connecting with people. I would always thrive on caring and on inspiring people to be more than they thought they could
be. But how was I to do that now that my leadership role was coming to an end? Moving into this next stage of life was harder than I'd
imagined it would be, and many of the lessons that are reflected in
these pages are what helped pull me through even though I had a
blessed life—a wife of 40-plus years, four children, and seven grandchildren, as well as abundant opportunities to travel around the globe.
Even so, I was lost at times, confused, unsure what would come next.

I have a lot to learn: One of the most important things I did was
to acknowledge that I did not have all the answers. I had to call out
questions, to myself and others. *What are my options to live with purpose? Can I be satisfied hanging out with my family and my seven incredible grandchildren as my main event? What else can I do to balance
my love of family with my love of being with my work colleagues? Who
would have me?* On and on the questions swirled in my mind.

I can't do it alone: I had learned long ago the freedom that comes from being authentic and vulnerable. And I knew there were people out there trained to help, who wanted to help. I hired two professional coaches. Overkill? Maybe. But I knew I couldn't do it alone. I needed help!

I want to be inclusive: I also brought many others into my journey. I needed my personal table to be inclusive in the same way I had invited many colleagues to my professional tables over the years. My spouse, of course, had to endure the endless questions and the week-to-week emotional roller coaster. My colleagues—people to whom I used to *tell*—were now listening and then kindly telling *me*. New-found friends shared their experiences on similar journeys. And my children helped me find clarification through their own wisdom.

One day, I returned home after a week on the road, visiting a southern US city in the context of racial-equity work and then flying to DC and Houston to give two speeches on the topic. I had engaged with many on that trip, sharing experiences and learnings in small, large, and huge groups. I had been pushed and challenged, and I was excited when I came home. My daughter and wife agreed that, after listening to me recount my week with heartfelt enthusiasm, I wasn't ready to quit working: "We would love you to be with us all the time, but that is not meant to be."

I appreciate small acts of kindness: We don't always know how new opportunities will affect us, and once I started working on this book, I discovered the beauty of small acts making a big impact. That included colleagues being willing to tell me their stories. Another generous occasion for me was a time when a very busy and successful managing director and partner booked time with me to talk. I assumed he wanted to run something by me. I was sure off—he had set up time to simply meet up and check in with me to see how I was doing and how I was feeling. Wow, was I touched! This meant the world to me.

As you can see, even as a 40-plus-year work veteran who had a great run, I am still figuring things out as I make my way forward. Sometimes it gets uncomfortable as I keep striving to contribute, to lead, to give. And when a sharp curve comes along, it gets even harder. But staying on the path, or finding new ones, is essential for professional and personal growth at any age and at any leadership—or life— level. No matter where we are on the leadership trajectory, we can all strive to evolve and grow by finding opportunities and by following some of the suggestions given here.

HOW TO MAKE CHANGES: INSIGHTS FROM SEVERAL LEADERS ON BEGINNING THE JOURNEY

These suggestions are ways for you to improve yourself to set the stage for acts of generosity. Unlike other acts, which have secondary benefit to you, these efforts will improve you so that you are better equipped to act in fullhearted ways for others.

Grow by Growing Others

Yes, you want to climb and grow, and to do this, I suggest you follow one of the BCG values that has guided me for many years: grow by growing others. I have watched leaders throughout my career, from my first job at a restaurant to my many roles at BCG and everything in between. Without question, those leaders who teamed up with their people, created a trusting and authentic relationship, and worked hard to develop their teams were the ones who grew the most, developed into effective leaders, and earned the promotions.

The others? Well. I recall a manager at Procter & Gamble who was all about himself. He hobnobbed with the bosses and was a loud, boisterous backslapper. He moved fast through three promotions . . . but then he was gone. "All about you," as he demonstrated, rarely works.

Growing by growing others can be challenging, and Christina Sistrunk said it's OK to lay out your frustrations with your team and seek to uncover theirs. Although it can be scary, it's what allows you to make progress: acknowledging the challenges with honesty and authenticity.

> I had a coach who pushed me on the point that I can be absolutely right *and* absolutely wrong. Right in the facts, wrong in my approach to solving the challenges with my teams. He taught me a lot about sharing and thinking about why, the impact you want, and how to be honest. He also urged me to consider the greater good, not just your own satisfaction. So many enter a new role and look for a cookbook on solving problems: What is step one, two, three? They hope they can pop on a new pair of glasses, and it will all be clear. This is simply not the case. Effective leadership takes experimentation, testing, listening, and understanding this is not about you. It is about the entire team, the organization, moving forward together.

Be Curious, Interested, and Relentless

The people whose stories are presented in this book are interested in others and are natural problem solvers. They're also curious about how things work; as insatiable learners, they want to understand things in a deep way, gaining wisdom from experts, people they work with, and mentors. They are continually developing themselves, not for the brass ring, per se, but for the sake of their own need to evolve.

Joanne Crevoiserat advised to listen and be curious: "It is not all about what you are doing in your box; you must understand how your work connects to the organization's goals, and how your work impacts others. The more you understand all the connections, the easier it will be for you to anticipate and solve problems. Likewise, the rate of failure goes up immeasurably when those connections are not made. Always strive to learn and seek to understand what you do not know."

Connect to Your Team to Drive Those Outcomes

You, of course, know you will be measured on results. While it is clear you must deliver, your chances are higher with an inspired and motivated team, and the better the connection to their leaders, the more motivated they will be.

Joaquin Duato put it plainly: "What you did, how hard you worked, how well you did in trying is all good, but it does not matter! As a leader, outcomes matter. This takes maturity. But the sooner you get it, the sooner you will step past yourself, listen to others, and connect more fully with your teams, and the sooner you will release, and be able to leverage, all the human traits critical to get positive results."

Joaquin believes that exceptional metrics, regular reporting, and great pay are also required to get your team to their best selves. The sooner you accept this starting point, the sooner you will start your own journey of elevating the heart in your leadership.

Seize Every Opportunity

Be the best you that you can be, so you can be better for others. Joaquin also said he never turned down an opportunity:

> I was once asked to move into a new business although I had hoped to be assigned head of Europe. I considered leaving, but I took it. It opened new windows, new doors, new opportunities.

I also learned a lot. I expanded; I grew. It tested my leadership skills, expanded my understanding of people, opened my mind to learning all I could from others. It also expanded my set of tools and skills I could use to motivate and inspire others. I believe one should never shy away from opportunities that allow us to learn and grow, to learn and perform.

Fran Katsoudas shared similar counsel as she looked back over her career: "I would strongly recommend that a younger me collect experiences. Be bold; do not hesitate. It is so natural to think everyone else has it figured out. The game is really all about learning. You have to trick yourself sometimes to let go of your insecurities, to change your frame of mind. I went against what the system was saying was valuable—promotion velocity—and instead I focused on elevating my team in every experience, in the end, this is what worked best for me and was most true to myself."

There are countless ways to develop yourself as long as you remain up for a challenge, open to a path you hadn't considered, willing to learn, and confident enough to lead. As high achievers, we are all accustomed to mapping our own trajectories, but leadership also requires humility, flexibility, agility, and the courage to take on those unexpected experiences that arise.

As I have told my children, it is OK to have a general plan, but be wary of being too specific. Fill it with aspiration and vision, and then be ready for the twists and turns—and when they come, grab the good ones.

CALL TO ACTION

How you start implementing these changes should fit within your available time and depend on what you prioritize and what is of most interest to you. Remember, making these changes is a process and not something you can readily tick off on a checklist. You may want to try one, or a couple, of the following three approaches to get started: finding an existing work challenge to test and build some of your skills, adopting a set of small gestures, or expanding your action allyship.

Find a Work Challenge

Trying to infuse all of these heart-leading traits at once in your day-to-day can be daunting—in fact, simply too much. Some take real emotional change on your part. Many take a lot of time. Others take a change in what may be long-hardened beliefs—for example, the value and safety of tough-love feedback. This is a lifetime journey for me and for all with whom I spoke. Pushing yourself in a real-life, real-time leadership moment is the only way you can really test and build many of these traits. Select a current leadership experience to start building the skills.

CALL TO ACTION

Think about a work effort you have underway today that involves a team approach to problem-solving, with you actively leading, and that also engages with others across the organization. Use it as a pilot to test some of your heart-led skills.

Begin by thinking through the skills mentioned throughout this book. What is not working well? Where can you modify your leadership practices? Prioritize one or more of these of highest interest to you and go after them by reviewing the relevant chapters and the lessons from our guest leaders. Review the "Call to Action" sections and identify how you can leverage your strengths to accelerate progress in the areas you have prioritized.

Implement Small Gestures Now

As the data report and every leader in this book believes, small gestures mean so much. They can truly jump-start heart-led leadership, whether you do or don't go after, at this moment, the bigger moves suggested throughout this book.

CALL TO ACTION

Review Chapter 7 and identify some small gestures you can implement to show personal recognition—to show that the people on your team matter. You might choose to do any of the following:

- Send emails or texts on birthdays.
- Send congratulatory notes upon promotions, particular successes of colleagues, or new sales each week.
- Send immediate handwritten thank-you notes whenever you're given a gift.
- Give highly personalized (simple) gifts for major milestones.

Be sure to set up a reliable process for executing these new practices so your efforts are systematic, fair, and equitable.

Expand Your Allyships

Supporting others is what this book is all about. Supporting those for whom you care and who are facing structural disadvantages is important and a deeply personal way to lead from the heart.

CALL TO ACTION

Expand your action allyship. Are you a mentor for someone or for several people who experience structural disadvantages? Or are there some in your organization who could use your allyship even if you aren't their direct mentor? Whether you have some relationships underway or plan to start, take this simple self-assessment to identify areas where you might change your practice to better lead from the heart.

- Do you spend time simply listening to the person you are supporting? Do you seek to understand their goals and aspirations? Do you know what they perceive as their biggest roadblocks where you can help make a difference?
- Do you hold yourself back and refrain from telling them what they should do?
- Do you see the person as an individual, not as a member of the group to which you assume they belong?
- Are you available to them in their moments of crisis?
- Have you explored with them where you can help create opportunities? Are you working to create those opportunities, opening doors, and helping them start to pave their own paths, while not doing it for them?
- Do you stick with them, as a coconspirator, when the pressure is against them?
- Are you giving them the time they need from you? Are you coaching with your top 5 percent?
- Are they making progress? If not, is there more you can do?

FINAL THOUGHTS

Our work lives and our nonwork lives continue to blur, and many of us have begun to bring heart-led leadership into the office. If you are keen, there are many ways for you to bring more heart-led leadership into your life. Take a work situation and use it to grow yourself. Watch the changes as they occur; watch the impact on your teams.

As you implement some of the ideas we have discussed here, I believe you will find a virtuous integration among your work life, your volunteer roles, your moments with friends, and your family life. As each of us leads and lives with deep care and compassion for others—supported by deep integrity—everyone around us benefits, and we benefit as well.

10

SOMETHING BIGGER

You are a leader, or on your way to becoming one. You are likely a good leader, with the aspiration to become great. But to become great is complicated. You need to develop a vision, guide with confidence, set a clear strategy and path, build an exceptional team, and ensure highly effective execution. And you need to lead with your heart, founded on clear values, deep care and compassion, and integrity. It's a lot.

This book began with the assumption that you have many of the essential leadership skills that you need to be successful, but that something is missing—that you need to build a more robust set of intangible skills to lead in a disruptive future where your workforce has a set of expectations for leadership that are completely different from those of the past.

As I discussed in the introduction, today's employees seek a deeper, more genuine connection to their colleagues and their leadership. They want to be recognized as people but also for their efforts and their achievements; they want to grow and develop in their own careers, and they want to work with people who want that for them. Today's expectations are based on recognizing humanity, acknowledging the fundamental importance of quality of life, and embracing true partnership.

Samir Bodas spoke to me about the changing expectations for leadership during his 30 years in business. Today's leaders must still deliver results but must operate from a purposeful foundation built on values, honesty, and integrity. "I saw this real time when I led my first turnaround. I took on a company that needed a reboot: the employees needed to believe in themselves and the company. We established clear values, and we worked hard to live up to those values. We led with truth, openness, vulnerability. We had authentic, open conversations, especially in vulnerable situations. The resultant benefits were clear: customers trusting us, better partnerships, much less friction across the team. It worked!"

Samir's experience is a living model of the work of this book—that leading with truth and openness creates tangible value, customer loyalty, stronger partnerships, and more cohesive teamwork.

I have a final powerful story to share with you about the necessary adaptability of leaders in our changing times. I recently spoke to Cristina Lilly, head of BCG BrightHouse North America, who told the story of an ex-military leader, now businessman, she was coaching. For years, in the military, he had learned, and led, as he was coached—in a command-and-control model. Absolutely necessary in that organization. As she was coaching him in his new role, suggesting actions that were more inclusive, listening behaviors that considered the opinions of others more meaningfully, he noted, "But, ma'am, I was one of those who walked the wall for you and this country; I do not know what to do now, how to adjust. Teach me."

Here was the face of the new business leader: trained in a historical model that had been essential to his previous role but was not fitting in his new role. That style fails to inspire today's employee and likely alienates them. His story is one of vulnerability and humility, an openness to change, and desire to learn. He recognized and admitted that he didn't know how to lead any other way than how he had been taught for 30-plus years—but he was willing to work hard to adapt and change. A simple, but incredibly powerful, first step required to evolve and transform.

Generous Leaders Have Integrity

To be a generous leader, you must live and lead with integrity, and Justin Dean is a first-rate example. Well respected for his contributions to his energy clients and his management of people within BCG in his role as Mid-Atlantic System lead, Justin is also highly appreciated for his leadership in racial equity within BCG and across the United States. He is an inspiring people leader *and* business leader who believes in the power of telling stories about yourself. One of his stories involves when he decided to cross his line, which he was compelled to do in the name of integrity—putting another first.

When did I cross my line? I had a very tough story I was keeping to myself: I basically bombed college. I failed to study, forgot it was college. Was simply doing too many other things. I carried this experience privately for a long time.

But life did change, and that experience was not the full me. Management Leadership for Tomorrow (MLT) is an organization that works with young Black individuals such as myself to build our confidence, open the world to the opportunities in which we might achieve, and help people like me pursue those opportunities. In the process, we are expected to pass our learning on. I met up with MLT, got a good GMAT score, and went on to Kellogg. That led to BCG. But I still kept my story secret.

You know when that changed? What the trigger was for me to cross my line? Injustice to another.

I was the office lead for the DC office, and we were debriefing our recruiting interviews. One candidate absolutely aced the

interviews but had a low GPA. The review team was having serious issues with the GPA, until I told my college story. In that
room, to about eight of my colleagues, I was now the "boss" feeling
an injustice about to happen to this candidate. So, I opened up.

It was freeing. It had taken me nine years at BCG, earning
promotions all the way to becoming managing director, partner,
and office lead—becoming the boss—until I was able to finally
open up. But even more importantly, it took an injustice about to
happen . . . when I saw someone about to be done wrong, for me
to cross my line.

Heart-led leadership with integrity has many words and phrases
attached to it; for Justin in this moment, it was about vulnerability,
putting another first, and doing what is right.

Change is hard. But if you are willing to be vulnerable, with a true
desire to learn (like the military leader), willing to lead with integrity and cross your own line when the moment comes to put another
first (like Justin), and willing to listen and lead with truth (as Samir
urged), you will transform the way you lead. You will inspire those
whom you lead, and collectively you will achieve more than you
imagined.

Generous Leaders Are Committed

I wake up each morning with 10 guiding actions that I hope will help
inform me as I engage with, and work to inspire, others—both personally and professionally.

1. Start the day caring.
2. Always remember I do not know what I do not know.
3. Find constant opportunities to engage, listen, and hear.

4. Work hard to hear from, and team with, the broadest possible set of voices.
5. Engage honestly; be real.
6. Speak plainly, directly, and honestly in all interactions.
7. Make decisions decisively, yet with the confidence and humbleness to adjust if wrong.
8. Make productive use of each moment each day.
9. Live each day positively, with high energy and a smile that exudes confidence.
10. Care for myself, my health, and my well-being (exercise, sleep, diet).

In addition to these guiding actions, I also add an extra one: practice *metta* meditation (loving-kindness meditation) a bit each day.

I believe these each have contributed to my life's track record. I also believe and hope they allow me to play my small part in making our world a better place.

Allow me to suggest that you take some time and articulate what guides you each day. Expand your own list where you see opportunities. Let your life's labor be one of uplifting others, do it well, and become one of the many ripples amplifying across a pond and elevating our world.

I hope you enjoyed this book. I hope you learned a thing or two. And I hope you start to apply some of your learnings now.

NOTES

Unless otherwise noted, quotes from business leaders and others are from personal conversations with the author.

Introduction

1. Kristin Peck, "We're in the Same Storm, but Our Boats Are Pretty Different," interview by Alan Murray, *Leadership Next* (podcast), *Fortune*, September 20, 2022, https://podcasts.apple.com/us/podcast/were-in -the-same-storm-but-our-boats-are-pretty-different/id1501891506?i =1000580035476.
2. Boston Consulting Group, *Human-Centered Leaders Are the Future of Leadership* (Boston Consulting Group, 2021).

Chapter 2

1. Craig Mullaney et al., *2022 Connected Leadership* (Brunswick Group, 2022), https://www.brunswickgroup.com/media/9905/connected-leader ship-2022-report.pdf.
2. John F. Helliwell et al., eds., *World Happiness Report 2021* (New York: Sustainable Development Solutions Network, 2021), https://world happiness.report/ed/2021/.
3. Erin Eatough, "The Resilient Bounce Back Stronger," BetterUp, February 24, 2021, https://www.betterup.com/blog/the-resilient-bounce -back-stronger.

4. "The Power of Three," Willis Towers Watson, May 7, 2016, https://www
.wtwco.com/-/media/wtw/insights/2016/02/willis-towers-watson-the
-power-of-three.pdf.

5. "COVID-19: A Message to Marriott International Associates from
President and CEO Arne Sorenson," YouTube video, 5:49, posted
March 20, 2020, https://www.youtube.com/watch?v=SprFgoU6aO0.

6. Carmine Gallo, "Marriott's CEO Demonstrates Truly Authentic Leadership in a Remarkably Emotional Video," *Forbes*, March 21, 2020,
https://www.forbes.com/sites/carminegallo/2020/03/21/marriotts
-ceo-demonstrates-truly-authentic-leadership-in-a-remarkably
-emotional-video/?sh=28dfd6241654.

7. Jim VandeHei, Mike Allen, and Roy Schwartz, *Smart Brevity: The Power
of Saying More with Less* (New York: Workman, 2022).

8. Adam Grant, *Originals: How Non-conformists Move the World* (New
York: Penguin Books, 2017).

Chapter 3

1. "Learn about Google's Manager Research," re:Work, accessed Au-
gust 28, 2023, https://rework.withgoogle.com/guides/managers-identify
-what-makes-a-great-manager/steps/learn-about-googles-manager
-research/.

2. Michael Platt et al., "Perspective Taking: A Brain Hack That Can Help
You Make Better Decisions," Knowledge at Wharton, Wharton School
of the University of Pennsylvania, March 22, 2021, https://knowledge
.wharton.upenn.edu/article/perspective-taking-brain-hack-can-help
-make-better-decisions/.

3. Speech given by the student body president at the Whitman College
Board of Trustees meeting, May 6, 2022.

Chapter 4

1. Gabrielle Novacek et al., *Inclusion Isn't Just Nice. It's Necessary* (Boston
Consulting Group, February 2023), https://web-assets.bcg.com/4c/ca
/dfd11bc1457a8668048a10606859/bcg-inclusion-isnt-just-nice.-It's
-Necessary_Feb-2023.pdf.

2. Tom Ziglar, *10 Leadership Virtues for Disruptive Times: Coaching Your Team through Immense Change and Challenge* (Nashville: Nelson Books, 2021).
3. Juliet Bourke, *Which Two Heads Are Better than One? How Diverse Teams Create Breakthrough Ideas and Make Smarter Decisions* (Sydney: Australian Institute of Company Directors, 2016).
4. Alex Gorsky, CEO speech given at the Chief Executives for Corporate Purpose board of boards meeting, November 14, 2022.
5. *Rewriting the Rules for the Digital Age: 2017 Deloitte Global Human Capital Trends* (Deloitte University Press, 2017).

Chapter 5

1. Nan DasGupta et al., "Small Actions, Big Impact: How to Be an Ally at Work and Why It Matters," BCG, November 24, 2020, https://www.bcg.com/en-ca/publications/2020/how-to-practice-allyship-foster-ally-culture.
2. Melinda Briana Epler et al., *State of Allyship Report: The Key to Workplace Inclusion* (Empovia, 2020), https://empovia.co/allyship-report/.
3. Rocío Lorenzo et al., "How Diverse Leadership Teams Boost Innovation," BCG, January 23, 2018, https://www.bcg.com/publications/2018/how-diverse-leadership-teams-boost-innovation.
4. Dame Vivian Hunt, Dennis Layton, and Sara Prince, "Why Diversity Matters," McKinsey & Company, January 1, 2015, https://www.mckinsey.com/capabilities/people-and-organizational-performance/our-insights/why-diversity-matters.
5. Marcus Noland, Tyler Moran, and Barbara Kotschwar, "Is Gender Diversity Profitable? Evidence from a Global Survey" (WP 16-3, Working Paper Series, Peterson Institute for International Economics, Washington, DC, February 2016), https://www.piie.com/sites/default/files/documents/wp16-3.pdf.
6. Patrick R. Grzanka, Jake Adler, and Jennifer Blazer, "Making Up Allies: The Identity Choreography of Straight LGBT Activism," *Sexuality Research and Social Policy* 12, no. 3 (2015): 165–81, https://doi.org/10.1007/s13178-014-0179-0.

7. Glenda M. Russell and Janis S. Bohan, "Institutional Allyship for LGBT Equality: Underlying Processes and Potentials for Change," *Journal of Social Issues* 72, no. 2 (2016): 335–54, https://doi.org/10.1111/josi .12169.

Chapter 6

1. Claire Hastwell, "Creating a Culture of Recognition," Great Place to Work United States, March 2, 2023, https://www.greatplacetowork.com /resources/blog/creating-a-culture-of-recognition.
2. Bob Anderson, *The Leadership Circle Profile: Breakthrough Leadership Assessment Technology* (Leadership Circle, n.d.), https://leadershipcircle .com/wp-content/uploads/2018/03/LCP_Breakthrough.pdf.
3. Dana Theus, "Feedback Coaching: How to Get Results with 'Tough Love,'" InPower Coaching, April 7, 2021, https://inpowercoaching.com /feedback-coaching/.
4. "Survey: Job Engagement Declines for a Third of Workers," Conference Board, October 18, 2022, https://www.conference-board.org/press /job-engagement-declines-for-third-of-workers.
5. Michelle Stohlmeyer Russell and Lori Moskowitz Lepler, "How We Closed the Gap between Men's and Women's Retention Rates," *Harvard Business Review*, May 19, 2017, https://hbr.org/2017/05/how-we -closed-the-gap-between-mens-and-womens-retention-rates.

Chapter 7

1. TINYPulse, *2014 TINYpulse Employee Engagement and Organizational Culture Report* (TINYPulse, 2014), https://www.tinypulse.com/landing -page-2014-employee-engagement-organizational-culture-report.
2. Jamie Gruman, "Small Gestures Make a Big Difference at Work," *Psychology Today*, February 7, 2020, https://www.psychologytoday.com/us /blog/dont-forget-the-basil/202002/small-gestures-make-big -difference-work.
3. Adam M. Grant and Francesca Gino, "A Little Thanks Goes a Long Way: Explaining Why Gratitude Expressions Motivate Prosocial Behavior," *Journal of Personality and Social Psychology* 98, no. 6 (2010): 946– 55, https://doi.org/10.1037/a0017935.

Chapter 8

1. Mark C. Crowley, "Why You Need to Lead with Your Heart," *Fast Company*, October 15, 2012, https://www.fastcompany.com/3002141/why-you-need-lead-your-heart.

2. Potential Project and the Human Leader, *Leaders Are Alarmingly out of Sync with Their Teams* (Potential Project and the Human Leader, 2022), https://global-uploads.webflow.com/5ff86e096165bce79acc825c/61d4d314d6b575a249a133b0_THL%20second%20edition.pdf.

3. Stephanie O. Lopez, "Vulnerability in Leadership: The Power of the Courage to Descend" (PhD diss., Seattle Pacific University, 2018).

4. Mary Kay Copeland, "The Impact of Authentic, Ethical, Transformational Leadership on Leader Effectiveness," *Journal of Leadership, Accountability, and Ethics* 13, no. 3 (2016): 79–97, https://fisherpub.sjf.edu/cgi/viewcontent.cgi?article=1038&context=business_facpub.

5. Emma Seppälä, "What Bosses Gain by Being Vulnerable," *Harvard Business Review*, December 11, 2014, https://hbr.org/2014/12/what-bosses-gain-by-being-vulnerable.

6. Sebastian Korb et al., "The Perception and Mimicry of Facial Movements Predict Judgments of Smile Authenticity," *PLOS One* 9, no. 6 (2014): e99194, https://doi.org/10.1371/journal.pone.0099194.

RESOURCE

SELF-ASSESSMENT

Dear reader: It was suggested to me that I should exclude this self-assessment, which covers some of the key points of each chapter all in one place. The risk was that you would pick up the book, find this at the back, and not bother to read the preceding chapters. I know. I also do this quite often while meandering through airport bookstores! But there are some great stories and anecdotes you will miss that may inspire you to action, so if you are one of those who are tempted to skip the main narrative, I do encourage you to stop and give the full book a read. But I am also willing to take the risk that you don't and make it easier for you to skim through many of my points. My ultimate goal is to encourage more of us to elevate the heart in our leadership, to be more generous leaders, so if this appendix piques your interest, you will still benefit. If you benefit, we all benefit.

For a quick summary of actions to lead more from the heart and explore how you are living each one, work through the list and score yourself in three simple buckets:

- I am doing well.
- I am doing OK but have opportunity for improvement.
- I do not really practice this trait/action.

I always find it useful to bounce my view of my performance off others—my spouse, my closest work confidants. It can be hard; I know I have to go into those conversations with a very open mind. Very often I do not like what I hear. If you wish, you might ask a trusted colleague, a friend, or your spouse/partner about how you're doing in relation to these questions. Be sure to listen to learn; these are their observations, whether you like them or not.

Finally, compare your self-assessment with their responses. Where are your biggest opportunities? Of those, where is your interest highest to make progress? OK . . . go after those!

BE SINCERE AND HONEST

- Do you convey your messages (in the appropriate time) with sincerity and honesty?
- Do you seek to tell the truth in the toughest of moments?
- Do others hear your messages as you mean them?
- Do you practice the "three-times" rule, repeating your messages, when the stakes are high?
- Do you leverage multiple tools to connect with your teams?
- Do you inject personal warmth and a bit of humor into your messages when you can?
- Do you test your messages and words with small groups of people who aren't part of your inner circle or with a trusted colleague?

SHOW RESPECT

- Do you have a general belief that there is much you do not know, even in your area of expertise?
- Are you curious about what is in others' minds?

- Do you believe others will add to your thinking if engaged?
- Do you ask for other people's views and opinions?
- Are you curious about others' lived experiences?
- Do you listen—a lot?
- Do you let the other person finish their point, their sentence?
- Before you engage with others, do you think through
  - their situation and what their point of view might be as you start to engage;
  - what they might want from the interaction;
  - what might make them pause or be nervous about your presence;
  - what they know, or might know, that you do not?
- Do you work to engage the skeptics and uncover the *no*s?

SHARE THE SPOTLIGHT

- Do you find that most of your advice and counsel meetings are only with your inner circle?
- Do you invite some of those who did the preparation to attend your review, strategy, and planning meetings?
- If you do:
  - Do you think in advance about what they could contribute?
  - Do you actively invite them into the conversation?
  - Are you supportive and encouraging to them if you can sense the pressure is high?

SHOW HUMILITY—BE AN ACTION ALLY

Do you have someone, or several people, from structurally disadvantaged experiences for whom you are a mentor? An ally?

If yes, are you pushing yourself to be a strong action ally?

- Do you spend time simply listening to the person? Understanding their goals and aspirations? Understanding their view on what they see as the biggest roadblocks where you can help open opportunities?
- Do you hold yourself back and resist jumping to the age-old "Let me tell you what to do"?
- Do you see the person as the person they are, not as part of the group to whom you assume they belong? Do you know their background—have you asked?
- Have you explored with them where you can help create opportunities? Are you working to create those opportunities, opening the door, starting to pave the path? Are you helping without doing the work for them?
- Do you stick with them, as a coconspirator, when the road gets bumpy?
- Are you there in their moments of crisis?
- Are you giving them the time they need? Are you giving your top 5 percent?
- Have you discussed with them whether they are making progress toward their aspirations? If not, is there more you can do—or is it on them?

VALIDATE

- Do you think about the person on your team and not the role the person is in?
- Do you think about what that person is contributing and what else they could contribute?
- Do you actively recognize your employees, especially for a job well done?

- In addition to thinking about your employees' development needs, do you also think deeply about their strengths and how they could leverage those strengths to work on their opportunities?
- Are you clear in feedback, *really*? Are you candid, honest, frank?
- Do you avoid sharing difficult feedback in the annual review that might surprise the employee because they haven't heard it before? Do you strive to give this difficult feedback throughout the year?
- Do you consciously think about and act on providing real-time feedback when you notice an opportunity to do so?

RECOGNIZE PEOPLE—PAY CLOSE ATTENTION

Do you regularly practice some, if not all, of these connecting gestures?

- Sharing a smile and saying hello.
- Greeting others by their names or repeating their names when introduced and using their names as you leave the event or meeting.
- Saying "thank you"—a lot.
- Openly talking about those who made a difference to you or who helped you along the way.

Do you maximize meeting moments to share humanity and connect with these simple gestures?

- Showing up on time for meetings or sending a note if you're going to be even two to three minutes late.

- Acknowledging every person in the room or on Zoom (as is practical) when you arrive.
- Asking those others may not know to introduce themselves.
- Sharing personal information about yourself and letting others into your life.
- Asking those who are less senior something about their lives in that moment.
- Starting Monday meetings by asking about everybody's weekends.
- Asking others to pronounce their name if it is not obvious to you.
- Resisting the urge to cancel a meeting without notice and strong reason.
- Being the first up in a large meeting, even when you are the most senior, to hand out refreshments.

Do you pay attention to what matters to others?

- Responding quickly, even if simply to acknowledge that you received their outreach and will respond more fully later.
- Sending an email or text on birthdays—or calling.
- Sending a congratulatory note upon promotion, for meaningful new sales, or when something else meaningful has been accomplished.
- Writing an immediate handwritten thank-you note whenever given a gift, or sending an email if you must.
- Looking for the special opportunities to give highly personalized gifts for major milestones.
- Sending a handwritten, personalized holiday card to everyone on your team (I know this is a big ask).

BE ACCESSIBLE

- Do you avoid appropriately sharing your personal life in the work setting?
- How do you react when others, above and below you, speak about their own personal situations at work? Do you listen?
- Do you worry about the perceptions of others if you discuss aspects of your life outside of work?
- Are you willing to say, "I do not know"?
- Do you acknowledge, aloud, when everyone is struggling to resolve a work challenge, including you?
- Do you speak out publicly when issues violate your or your organization's values?
- Do you speak honestly in moments of crisis?

BE BETTER, TOWARD SOMETHING BIGGER

- Do you have a set of work and life principles that guide you each day?
- Do you know them? Do you think through whether you are living them?

ACKNOWLEDGMENTS

When I was 15 years old, I created a list of life goals. I had, among those goals, "to be published." I do not recall writing that, nor for many years did I ever imagine I would write a book, but here I am. As for everyone who finishes such an endeavor, there are so many who were critical to the journey.

I would like to start by thanking Marni Seneker, my book coach. Without her support, her encouragement, her motivation, and, more importantly, her sincere caring and her deep probing into what I was trying to say, it would never have been. Marni has become, not surprisingly, a dear friend—I cannot thank her enough. Then to Debbie Lovich, BCG colleague and friend, who constantly told me, "Joe, you have to write a book! You need to share your view on leadership." After my experience leading BCG North America through the COVID-19 pandemic, Debbie pushed me even harder. Debbie, in your positively persistent way, you got me going—thank you. I also want to call out another very dear friend and BCG colleague, Brian Gross. Brian also kept me going on my book effort. But, far more meaningfully, over the nine years that we worked together Brian helped me deepen my skills and efforts to lead generously from my heart.

A thank-you to the business leaders inside and outside BCG who shared their personal stories to help form my thinking for this book and give each of us a glimpse into your generous style of leadership. And, finally, I would be remiss if I did not call out the friends and colleagues from BCG over the years who did so much to form the leader I have become.

A huge thank-you to those at my publisher, Berrett-Koehler, who helped make this a reality. In particular I want to thank Jeevan Sivasubramaniam, Neal Maillet, Ashley Ingram, Sarah Nelson, and the entire BK team, for all they did to help and support along the way.

And to two very busy individuals who generously gave of their hearts and time to provide my manuscript a deep read-over and edit—Ken Keen, a dear friend who found time out of a very busy work life to do the first edit, and Gail Kretchmer, my first development editor, who, without question, made this book a much better read.

I would also like to thank the team from Girl Friday Productions who partnered with me initially to get this effort off the ground, as well as Ken Gillett and the team at Target Marketing Digital and Mark Fortier and the team from Fortier Public Relations for all their support.

And then to those dear friends who have meant so much for years. In particular, Steve Gunby, who is quoted throughout the book, a dear friend and mentor, who did so much to help me grow as a businessperson and a leader. Without Steve, the opportunity to develop my heart-led style would likely not have come.

To my children—Sadie, Hannah, Rebecca, and Andrew—who each kept me honest, focused, and on track, throughout life and through this book effort.

Then to my very dear friend and colleague Mary Kate Steincke, who teamed with me each day throughout my BCG North America regional chair journey. Mary Kate was also with me in each moment of this book's development, coming up with new ideas, finding content, and always encouraging me.

Finally, of course, my wife, Sarah. Sarah and I have partnered together the past 44 years. Sarah encouraged me every step of the way, from the very early days, when she told me not to quit as a Procter & Gamble sales rep, something I considered on many an occasion, telling me, "Joe, getting promoted a few times with P&G will mean so much to your future." How did she know that at age 24? She was also there during each BCG setback, reminding me, "All will be fine; just keep your chin up; do not let it get to you; keep at it." But most importantly, as anyone who knows Sarah knows, she taught me what it is to listen, to accept, to live each day from the heart, which is what she has been doing since she was old enough to connect with her fellow humans.

Thank you to each of you!

—Joe Davis

INDEX

ABOUT THE AUTHOR

Joe Davis is a managing director and senior partner at the Boston Consulting Group.

In *The Generous Leader*, Joe tells a story about a performance review from early in his career: to summarize, he was told he is not the best at problem solving in a vacuum but, in collaboration with others, can solve any challenge. Why? Because early in Joe's career this mentor identified his key strength—Joe was a person who could connect with anyone.

This ability to connect with people became the foundation of a successful career at BCG, spanning more than 35 years, opening and growing offices, starting businesses, and helping to grow the firm. Joe ultimately led BCG North America, including during the trying times of the COVID-19 pandemic. For more than three decades, Joe's passion for people and his desire to support their development inspired teams to work harder and better than they thought possible, creating exceptional collaborative results for BCG and its clients.

In keeping with his constant commitment to champion people and their dreams, Joe currently serves as chair of BCG's Center for Inclusion and Equity. He is a cofounding steering committee member of CEO Action for Diversity and Inclusion and the Southern Communities Initiative.

Joe is a graduate of Whitman College and currently serves as chair of the board of trustees. He previously served as vice chair of B Capital Group. He earned an MBA from Harvard Business School.

Joe has benefited from the generosity of a loving family: Sarah, his wife of more than 40 years, whom he met at Whitman College; his four children and their partners; and eight grandchildren.

Berrett–Koehler
BK Publishers

Berrett-Koehler is an independent publisher dedicated to an ambitious mission: *Connecting people and ideas to create a world that works for all.*

Our publications span many formats, including print, digital, audio, and video. We also offer online resources, training, and gatherings. And we will continue expanding our products and services to advance our mission.

We believe that the solutions to the world's problems will come from all of us, working at all levels: in our society, in our organizations, and in our own lives. Our publications and resources offer pathways to creating a more just, equitable, and sustainable society. They help people make their organizations more humane, democratic, diverse, and effective (and we don't think there's any contradiction there). And they guide people in creating positive change in their own lives and aligning their personal practices with their aspirations for a better world.

And we strive to practice what we preach through what we call "The BK Way." At the core of this approach is *stewardship,* a deep sense of responsibility to administer the company for the benefit of all of our stakeholder groups, including authors, customers, employees, investors, service providers, sales partners, and the communities and environment around us. Everything we do is built around stewardship and our other core values of *quality, partnership, inclusion,* and *sustainability.*

This is why Berrett-Koehler is the first book publishing company to be both a B Corporation (a rigorous certification) and a benefit corporation (a for-profit legal status), which together require us to adhere to the highest standards for corporate, social, and environmental performance. And it is why we have instituted many pioneering practices (which you can learn about at www.bkconnection.com), including the Berrett-Koehler Constitution, the Bill of Rights and Responsibilities for BK Authors, and our unique Author Days.

We are grateful to our readers, authors, and other friends who are supporting our mission. We ask you to share with us examples of how BK publications and resources are making a difference in your lives, organizations, and communities at www.bkconnection.com/impact.

Dear reader,

Thank you for picking up this book and welcome to the worldwide BK community! You're joining a special group of people who have come together to create positive change in their lives, organizations, and communities.

What's BK all about?

Our mission is to connect people and ideas to create a world that works for all.

Why? Our communities, organizations, and lives get bogged down by old paradigms of self-interest, exclusion, hierarchy, and privilege. But we believe that can change. That's why we seek the leading experts on these challenges—and share their actionable ideas with you.

A welcome gift

To help you get started, we'd like to offer you a **free copy** of one of our bestselling ebooks:

www.bkconnection.com/welcome

When you claim your **free ebook**, you'll also be subscribed to our blog.

Our freshest insights

Access the best new tools and ideas for leaders at all levels on our blog at ideas.bkconnection.com.

Sincerely,

Your friends at Berrett-Koehler

Certified

Corporation